Past Poets - Future Voices

2010 Poetry Competition for 11-18 year-olds

Visions Of Youth

Edited by Vivien Linton & Jonathan Fisher

First published in Great Britain in 2010 by

 Young**Writers**

Remus House
Coltsfoot Drive
Peterborough
PE2 9JX
Telephone: 01733 890066
Website: www.youngwriters.co.uk

All Rights Reserved
Book Design by Ali Smith & Tim Christian
© Copyright Contributors 2010
SB ISBN 978-0-85739-194-0

Foreword

Young Writers was established in order to promote creativity and a love of reading and writing in children and young adults. We believe that by offering them a chance to see their own work in print, their confidence will grow and they will be encouraged to become the poets of tomorrow.

Our latest competition 'Past Poets - Future Voices' was specifically designed as a showcase for secondary school pupils, giving them a platform with which to express their ideas, aspirations and passions. In order to expand their skills, entrants were encouraged to use different forms, styles and techniques.

Selecting the poems for publication was a difficult yet rewarding task and we are proud to present the resulting anthology. We hope you agree that this collection is an excellent insight into the voices of the future.

Contents

Srijita Chattopadhyay (17) 1
Taymara Clarke (13) 2
Aye-Marie Conteh (12) 2
Talwyn Edwards (13) 3

Aith Junior High School, Shetland
Katy Shewan (14) 3
James Cree-Hay (13) 4
Allie Clubb (13) 6
Rhona Moar (13) 7

Bentley Wood High School, Stanmore
Sadeqa Jagani (14) 8
Samlya Scannell (14) 10
Kinnari Naik (15) 11
Deanna Phillips (15) 12
Hannah Nathanson (15) 13
Laraib Sohail (14) 14
Sulkha Abdi (15) 15
Sana Bhatia (13) 16
Sammi Waters (14) 17

Bo'ness Academy, Bo'ness
Daniel Weir (13) 17
Hannah Speirs (13) 18
Lauren Baillie (12) 18
Ross Monaghan (12) 19
Kelly Bissett (12) 19
Amber Paterson (12) 20
Courtney Wilson (13) 20
Chloe Paterson (12) 21
Shanagh Penman (13) 21
Matthew Cullen (12) 22
Ellie Williams (12) 22
Jamie Argent (12) 23
Lauren Stupart (12) 23
Joanna Bissett (12) 24
Connor Earle (12) 24

Jordan Sharp (12) 25
Natasha Cameron (12) 25
Matthew Martin (13) 26
Laura Quigley (13) 26
Meghan Fraser (13) 27
Steven Graham (12) 27
Hayley Calvert (12) 28
Rebecca Johnstone (12) 28

Chadwell Heath Foundation School, Romford
Saleha Iftikhar (12) 28
Zahrah Sheikh (18) 29
Migle Mickeveciute 30
Hannah Puri (12) 31
Aisha Dowlut (13) 32
Reema Chandarana (12) 33
Mohammed Ruhel Amin (12) 34
Samuel-Eliud Muturi (12) 35
Rawdah Mahmood (12) 36
Nadia Patel (11) 37
Sanjeet Dhinsa (12) 38
Navnit Dhaliwal (12) 39
Chris Adebayo (12) 39
Amar Ladva (12) 40
Sadiyah Jaffar (12) 41
Rayan Shah (11) 42
Vinuri Vithanage (11) 43
Yanick Adjoumani (12) 43
Simran Mahil (12) 44
Summer Peters (12) 44
Samaha Uddin (12) 45
Emily Shah (11) 45
Vithusan Jeevarajan (12) 46
Zainab Ahmed (12) 46
Rachel Dinnes (11) 47
Bobby Curley (11) 47
Jordan La Touche (11) 48
Kumari Shyllon-Webb (11) 48

Anneka Patel (15) 49
Sharanga Thuvaraganathan (11) 49
Francesca Burr (12) 50
Jade Wood (15) 50
Aliba Haque (12) 51
Monique Reddock (12) 51
Haroon Ikram (15) 52
Prabhjit Singh (15) 52
Saira Arshad (11) 53
Ross Dipple (11) 53
Michael Jordan (11) 54
Navreet Dhaliwal (12) 54
Naveed Ur Rahman (12) 55
Chlöe Brown (12) 55
Noreen Pokun (12) 56
Kori Meikle (12) 56
Aliza Alam (13) 57
Nicole Johnson (12) 57

Dunluce School, Bushmills

Charlene Hardy (14) 57
Anna Thompson (14) 58
Abbie Harte (14) 59
Kyra McLaughlin (14) 60
Ellen Devenney (13) 60
Jessica Harris (14) 61
Arianne Stirling (12) 61
David Fillis (13) 62
Kyle McLelland (12) 62
Sara Dallat (14) 63
Chelsea O'Doherty (12) 63
Jordan Ramage (14) 64
Kelly McKissick (13) 64
Catherine Duclayan (14) 65
Cathy Hogg (14) 65
Rebecca Knowles (12) 66
Joshua McCartney (14) 66
Chloe Freeman & Sophie Keys (14) .. 67
Brent Smith (14) 67
Luke Philpott (13) 68
Amy O'Brien (14) 68
Alex O'Neill (13) 69
Abbie Dunlop (14) 69

Stefanie Patton (12) 70
Aaron Agnew (12) 70
Johnathan McGowan (12) 71
Billy Grant (12) 71
David Kelly (11) 72
Tanith Speers (14) 72
Matthew Nicholl (13) 72
Brad Moore (12) 73
Jack Milligan (12) 73
Bradley Barber (12) 74
Christopher Macauley (12) 74
Owen Black (12) 75
Nicole Brown (14) 75
Craig Nelson (12) 76
Melissa Duncan (12) 76
Lauren Williamson (13) 76
Melissa Rainey (13) 77
Regan White (13) 77
Bethany Hannah (12) 77
Steven Lyons (13) 78
Dylan McKendry (12) 78
Jamie McKee (13) 78
Hannah McClarty (12) 79
Ben Walker (13) 79

St Peter's School, Bournemouth

Kane West (13) 79
Olivia Arnaudy (13) 80
Zoe Mundell (13) 84
Annabelle Buckfield (13) 87
Lois Rawlins (13) 88
Charlotte Wragg (12) 91
Thomas Greenfield (13) 92
Sinead Tickner (12) 95
Lilith Riley (13) 96
Danielle Magnien (12) 98
Rhianna Metcalfe (13) 100
Bethany Emerton (12) 101
Daniel Nascimento 102
Patrick McManus (12) 104
Andrew Sackett (13) 106
Ellen Higgins (13) 108
Gianpiero Placidi (13) 110

Yasmin Reid (13) 112
James Flynn (13) 113
Sharon Thompson (13) 114
Francesca Whitaker (12) 115
Samantha Keating (13) 116
Michael Laking (13) 117

Skinners' Kent Academy, Tunbridge Wells

Abi Harmsworth (14) 118
Holly Martin (13) 119
Daniel Barrett (13) 120
Charlotte Taylor (11) 121
James Jenner (13) 121
Bethan Pierce (14) 122
Brogan Malyon (14) 122
Jordan Wilson (12) 123
Geordie Starling (13) 124
Chantelle Streeter (12) 125
Charlie Brooker (13) 126
Rhys Watts (11) 126
Ellie Brooker (13) 127
Joshua Hamilton (12) 127
Francesca Drewett (12) 128
Kelsey-Marie Stanford (12) 128
Jasmine Gower (12) 129
Summer Woodcraft (11) 129
Lliam Grant (12) 130
Jacob Court (11) 130
Paige Clark (12) 131
Jack Attwater (12) 131
Yasmeen Soudani (14) 132
Lucy Bickmore (12) 132
Casey Ansell (12) 133
Harry Clark (12) 133
Ria Sellings (12) 134
Katie Gough (12) 134
Sasha Fry (12) 135
Georgia Rayner (13) 135
Meghan Edwards (12) 136
Ellie Maynard (12) 136
Shifaul Ahmed (14) 137
Holly Wright (14) 137
Holly Freeman (13) 138
Martina Cooper (12) 138

The Knights Templar School, Baldock

Kayla Ellis (12) 139
Bethany Welch (14) 140
Adam Lunnon (13) 142
Lauren Marshall (12) 143
Becky Ludbrook (12) 144
Tom Picking (14) 145
James Hazzard (12) 146
Tahja Grimes (14) 147
Callum Dungey (12) 147
Matthew Dyne (12) 148
Katie Harbon (15) 149
Athen Wilton-Wright (13) 150
Eleana Bull (13) 151
Megan Pain (12) 152
Emily Fisher (12) 153
Amy McCarthy (12) 154
Kate Bennett (12) 155
Karen Pritchett (11) 156
Calum Brooker (14) 157
Harry Goddard (12) 158
Harry Morris (12) 158
Daniel Maynard (12) 159
Callum Duffy (12) 159
Laura Overton (11) 160
Robin Peters (12) 160
Sasha Giovine (12) 161
Rosie Anderson (12) 161
Zoe Melabianaki (12) 162
Aisling Geoghegan 162
Natalie Smith (12) 163
Alexander Bandy (12) 163
Luke Geaves (14) 164
George Fryer (12) 164
Storm Cook (13) 165
Jody Margetson (12) 165
Alfie Laughton 166
Danni Malyon (11) 166
Sam Tomlinson (11) 167
Rosie Lord (13) 167
Matty Welander 168

Nicholas Bell (11) 168
Katie Winzer (12) 169
Rosie Barker (11) 169
Anna Docking (12) 170
Denver Tuck (11) 170
Sophie Hazzard (14) 171
Amelia Ellis 171
Aidan Tilbury & Max Johnson (14) ... 172
Helen Inman (12) 172
Jason Doherty 173
Jemma Fairey (12) 173
Jason Coyne (11) 174
Montana Strachan (12) 174
Jake Smith (11) 175
Imogen Hornby (12) 175
Rajvir Singh Jagpal (14) 176
Stuart Dougal (11) 176
Emma Nicholson (12) 176
Serena Harmsworth (12) 177
Carris Lee (13) 177
Sophie Hornblower (12) 177
Joe Nelson (11) 178
Daisy Flynn (12) 178
Holly Hayes (12) 178
Jack Smith (12) 179
Michael Fairburn (13) 179

Uplands Community College, Wadhurst
Tamsin English (13) 179
Jade Berry (13) 180
Sofie Fairweather (12) 180
Elliott Wallis (12) 181
Ian Lim (12) 181

The Poems

On The Eve

Beneath the deep blue sky
Of a winter's night,
I see the lulled town through
The frosted window of our house.
In the quietness of the night,
I hear him breathe
As he turns to the side
And snuggles next to me, asleep.
I stare at his calm, boyish face
And it reminds me of the day we first met.
Days, weeks, months and a year have gone away,
Yet it feels like I fell in love with him just yesterday.
Every breath he breathes
Floods me with memories from our past.
I slowly drift back to the day we first held hands,
The day we first hugged, the day we first kissed,
The day we first fought,
To the day we sat together and cried our pains out.
The spell of the past is suddenly broken . . .
As the clock strikes three,
Reminding me to lay down and sleep.
I rest my head over the pillow
And turn over the other side to set the alarm.
I suddenly feel his strong, warm hands, holding me near
As he lifts a lock of hair and puts it behind my ear
And whispers quietly,
'Will you be my valentine now and forever?'

Srijita Chattopadhyay (17)

The Odd One Out

These people want to get in, in with the crowd
But no one will let them, seems like they're not allowed
Amy wonders if people don't like her because she is white
Sam asks, 'If I am black does that mean I'm not right?'
Georgia asks why people bully her at school
She wonders, if I am too dumb, does that mean I'm not cool?
Mark's teacher says to him that he doesn't look well
It's because he's anorexic and people make his life hell
The teachers wonder what they can possibly do,
If they think something's wrong he will say, 'That's not true'
At every corner they must hide
And all they can do is cry inside
A lot of things can go on in someone's mind
And for them, the good things are too hard to find
In Ben's confidence there is now a dent
He wonders why he deserves such punishment
And even though these people are down all the time
When they open their mouth they insist they're fine
They want to tell people, they want to shout!
But they wouldn't be heard because they're the odd one out.

Taymara Clarke (13)

Elements Of The Earth

Moon, guide my path
Stars, show the way
Sun, tell the time
Until it reaches day

Sky, teach the clouds
Sea, bring memories
Stones, listen closely
And keep protecting me.

Aye-Marie Conteh (12)

Nature

Nature is our beauty
It shines with wildlife and plants
There are loads of places to see wildlife and plants
But now they're dying because of
Our pollution and getting rid of their habitats
What have we done to the world?
It's so horrible.

Talwyn Edwards (13)

Perfect Day

A sunny day on the beach
Suntan just in reach
A young girl sits under an umbrella
Her name is Ella
The waves are gentle against the rocks
Just like Ella's locks
The sun begins to set in the sea
Ella's dog jumps in the water, her name is Misty
Misty runs towards Ella with speed
She has something in her mouth, seaweed
Ella laughs at her friend
As the day slowly ends.

Katy Shewan (14)
Aith Junior High School, Shetland

Plane

All was sunny on that day
The day when it happened
There were the usual safety checks
Then along to the lounge

Down the air bridge single file
For the large steel box
We stowed away our luggage
And prepared to sit down

Then it happened so very quick
I was thrown off my feet
The fire started so ragingly fast
I barely had time to think

Then the smoke filled up the cabin
And I started to choke
Heat was creeping closer
Right up to my toes

I thought only of family
And survival all the while
As I ran to the exit
And out the small white door

I was knocked to the clean, cold ground
And saw the vehicles race by
With lights all flashing bright
And then up the pristine floor

The soot was falling off me
Then a boom, boom, boom
Then the earth was shaken
And another fell from the sky

I knew it was the very end
My life finished at last
The bodies lay around me
The skin all red and charred

The object changed direction
Heading left instead of right
It hit the other building
Tore through it like air

I made a great loud squeak
I had nowhere to run
I was trapped like a rat
Prepared to die

I was fixed on that very spot
I couldn't think straight
I'd never been more fearful
In my whole, entire life.

James Cree-Hay (13)
Aith Junior High School, Shetland

Nazi Flag

I sat there in my window sill
Looking out the night was still
Red flags flying everywhere
Flapping in the cold night air

Now a bleak, cold, scary place
Families stolen without a trace
Houses emptied, burned to ash
Happiness destroyed in one red flash

Nazi flag and Star of Jew
End to it long overdue
All their lives are full of doom
Endless, cruel, silent gloom

Suddenly the night is loud
With sirens like a large black cloud
The sound of shouting, just next door
They've never come so close before

Now so close I hear their words
Screaming, shouting, angry birds
Shoving us towards a van
All part of their evil plan

The van is crowded, full of fright
Charging through the cold, dark night
Fear is rising, children cry
In this horrid place we lie

Kicking us out of the van
A scary, shouting, angry man
Packing us into a room
Full of people, full of doom

Slowly silence creeping in
People dropping, small and thin
Now the room is dark and still
Lives destroyed, against their will.

Allie Clubb (13)
Aith Junior High School, Shetland

Amy Poem

It was a warm summer's day
As Amy walked into the church,
She remembered that cruel day,
The day Tracy had died.

The day Tracy was taken,
She was only 11.
Amy hadn't slept since.
Every time she shut her eyes,
She saw Tracy fall,
She heard Tracy scream.
She thought of the cliff,
The cliff Tracy had fallen off.

Amy still heard the splash of water,
Every day, every night.
Amy cried all through the funeral,
At the end her throat was dry.

Amy walked through the park,
She was cold, shaking.
As she looked over the edge of the cliff,
She saw the water below.
She felt sick,
The waves were as high as mountains.

Amy crawled back from the edge,
She thought of Tracy's scream.
She thought it was her fault Tracy had died.

Amy stood up and walked forwards,
Over the edge of the cliff,
Splash.

Rhona Moar (13)
Aith Junior High School, Shetland

My Dream As A Little Girl In The War . . .

I'm only a little girl, a very little girl with a very big dream!
A dream to see this atrocious war end, for this Great War
to just stop,
For everyone worldwide to become a big, united team,
Quality for everyone where no country is at the top,
The smiles on children's faces worldwide to glow
in one big bright beam,
I wish this war could just go pop!

Men are dying, being brutally killed on the front lines,
friends are now foes,
Everyone is fighting; they are all just as bad,
Bullets, guns, artillery of all sorts, trenches, the freezing cold
and frozen toes,
I think this world has gone mad.
Why is it that war has sent Daddy packing?
Why is it that war has sent Mummy working?
Why is it that I've been left so alone?
I don't want to moan and groan!

I don't know if my dad's alive, he went off with good old
Uncle Clive,
He said, 'It'll just be like a fun long dive.'
But I could see Mummy tearing up, I knew Daddy was lying.
Now he's stuck in a trench somewhere, starving, cold
and in a lot of pain,
I can imagine him running around, helping everybody
survive the bullet rain!
Mummy thinks I don't understand but believe me, I do,
I can see it in everyone's eyes, the thought of him dying;
they think I have no clue.

When I look around I don't see what I used to see through
my brown little eyes,
I see chaos, people hurrying home, everyone looks tense
and worried.
I just think back to those times I used to see every little girl
with their daddy,
Couples staring into each other's eyes.

Now all the soldiers stare at are the eyes of dead bodies.
Mummy tries to take control, she does her best but I still hear her tender cries.

I want Daddy to come home, I want to be able to go on holiday to Rome.
I want everything to go back to how it was,
I don't want Mummy to become a yellow canary, nor Daddy to be wounded,
I want everything back to how it was.

I am a little girl, a very little girl with a very big dream,
A dream to see all the little girls and boys back with their daddies and brothers,
To smell clean fresh air filled with my brother's aftershave in my bedroom,
To feel no more tears from any mothers,
So see those lovely little smiles loom.

Sadeqa Jagani (14)
Bentley Wood High School, Stanmore

World War I - It's All Over Now

You can't see where you are going,
You are blinded by the lack of light.
You have hundreds of soldiers marching in front of you.
In the trenches you have been walking for miles
And if you take your boots off,
You won't be able to get them back on again.
The thing you fear most is trench-foot
And when the weather gets warmer
Your feet will start to defrost.

Hang in there, it will all be over soon,
And it's all for the good of your country.
So come along lads, come and have fun,
It's all for the good of World War I.

No sleep, no eat, cold feet, no heat.
The only thing you can hear is bombs going off.
Your doctor says you will go deaf from the sound of guns.
Dark, wet, cold, nobody to hold.
The smell of rats is worse than death.
Mince pies, roast beef, and curry and rice,
Potato and fish and gravy, I wish!

Squashed feet, no meat, no seat, what can it beat?
Sitting on the cold, wet mud trying to warm yourself up,
Wondering when this is gonna end.
No wash for days.
Be careful out there, anything could happen,
You look over your shoulder, you can hear the captain.

You hope you will be able to go home soon
And get a single night's sleep in weeks.
Your family miss you and wonder
If you are going to come back alive.

Hang in there, it will all be over soon,
And it's all for the good of your country.
So come along lads, come and have fun,
It's all for the good of World War I.

No matter how bad it is, we all went through it,
We had good days and we had our bad days

10

But got our families back in the end.
Not the worst experience, not the best,
Though there was some pretty rancid stuff,
But it's all over now.

Samlya Scannell (14)
Bentley Wood High School, Stanmore

Keeping It In

I used to keep it all in,
Bottled up inside me,
Taking no notice,
As if I didn't care.

But in my heart I felt worthless,
The name calling got to me,
I used to cry and cry,
But lie and lie.

When I finally let it out,
It made me want to scream and shout,
Telling someone about the hurt and pain,
And how I was put to shame.

Telling someone made me feel better,
As if it didn't matter,
Knowing that someone cared,
The feeling had been very rare.

At the end I felt sorry,
Not for me,
But for she who called me names,
For she must be going through shame
To cause others pain.

I used to keep it all in,
Bottled up inside me,
Taking no notice,
As if I didn't care . . .

Kinnari Naik (15)
Bentley Wood High School, Stanmore

My First True Love

When I see you, my heart stops
I can see me and you together forever
Morning till night you're in my mind
This is my true love I hoped I would find
Our passion comes from within
Your beautiful soul is mine
Boy, in your eyes I see the sunshine

Forever and ever, yes indeed
Your hold, your touch
You drive me crazy thinking about our relationship
Dreams I have cause my heart to stop
Oh my true love, you are
Please believe no one else has made me sprung
Especially as we are so young

I thought I fell in love before you
Only I was stupid, now I realise
Things have made me grow up since
If you can take me as your princess, I'll take you as my prince
Feeling empty when you're far
I didn't plan to find someone like you yet
But I guess I'm trapped, I fell in your net

Hopefully there will be a future for us
A family to raise together forever
We are each other's backbone
Both as strong as a diamond throne
Whatever happens, I pray we're happy together
Although times will arise when we argue and fight
We'll always make up by the night

I'm sorry for all those who have been heartbroken
Please believe there is hope
For those who have been lied to
For those who do not know quite what to do
Remember Jesus in your life
As, if you never find a true love as have I
Your Lord, the Saviour, will never die.

Deanna Phillips (15)
Bentley Wood High School, Stanmore

Who Are We Learning For?

Who are we learning for?
Is it for the teachers, who are dropping
From their mound of work to mark?
Is it for our parents, whose voices are hoarse
From screaming at us over work not done
That our teachers can't mark?
Is it for the exam board, who write us gruelling tests
So our parents can scream more at us
Over the stack of work we haven't done
That out teachers can't mark?
Is it for the government, who whispers to the newspapers
To poke the exam board to write us harder tests
So our parents can scream more at us
Over the stack of work we haven't done
That our teachers can't mark?

Or is it for us?
They say they do it all for us,
That they're preparing us for the future.
That it's a harsh world,
A cruel world,
A world full of guns and violence.
So to teach us those lessons we are
Pressurised by tests that no one wants to write.
We are screamed at by parents
Who would rather keep their voice.
We are laden with detentions
That teachers don't want to sit through.

The government will get our tax.
The newspapers will get your money.
Who's it really for?
I had better hopes for the future . . .

Hannah Nathanson (15)
Bentley Wood High School, Stanmore

Pain

The dark clouds shield the light from the sky.
The warmongers charge towards us like a swarm of flies,
thirsty for us all to die.
Their monstrous faces staring through my sparkled blue eyes,
Our lieutenant shouts, 'Get ready guys!'
We all know we have no hope; lives will be lost on both of
the front lines,
There's no turning back, we either do or die.
They open fire, not knowing who to aim at,
I gasp and my voice echoes as I see my friend slowly die.
I see his tears revolve and run down his cheek.
Looking down the trench I see many of my fellow soldiers
Falling to the ground, screaming in the mud-baked walls.
The adrenaline rushes through my veins.
My hands pull on the rifle trigger,
The skin about my bones,
The soft labouring of my lungs,
And the hot, white, inward turning anger of my eyes rages
for vengeance of my fallen friends.
As I stand up with confidence,
I suddenly feel a force piercing through my body;
I drop to my knees,
The sight I see slowly turns into black.
After twenty hours, the peace of understanding on each face,
More candles, more lanterns, and more endless rain.
Those who do not understand true pain can never understand
true peace.

Laraib Sohail (14)
Bentley Wood High School, Stanmore

The Silent Killer

Many years have passed
But the biggest threat still lurks
Deep within the rocks undetected,
Causing pain and misery
Along its destruction-filled path,
Taunting and tricking unfortunate people to give up.
Poverty has struck again.

The beautiful ducklings are robbed
Of their freedom to fly
And explore the wonders of the world.
Instead they are left with the
Dry hole they call home.
They are deprived of their right to joy
As the other ducks watch and enjoy.
Lost in dreams they can't employ.
Poverty has struck again.

Exiled to an eternal cycle of doom,
Life could not bring a bigger burden,
Wishing their memories could be burned.
As they dreamed of equality for everyone, the ideal,
They were soon hit in the face by reality
Because it was not real.
Poverty has struck yet again.

Sulkha Abdi (15)
Bentley Wood High School, Stanmore

My WWI Wartime Poems

T renches are a horrible place to be in
H uddles of people cramped together
E nough is enough

T roubled by the sergeants
R ats eat our food
E ventually
N ot all of us will survive
C hildren will be sad
H ope I stay alive

T he soldier has no say
H e has to do everything he is told to
E ach day seems like a year

S eldom happy
O ther soldiers lead a horrible life
L ife has just gone down
D reading every day
I ntelligence is what I need
E nough is enough
R acing for his life.

Sana Bhatia (13)
Bentley Wood High School, Stanmore

Why Me?

Why me that got chosen?
Why me that lost my limbs?
Why me that had to do it?
Why me that had to risk my life?
Why me?

Why me that had to go in the trenches?
Why me that lost my boots?
Why me that got trench-foot?
Why me that couldn't sleep well?
Why me?

Why me? I may never get to see my little girl.
Why me? My wife is worrying.
Why me? My family is scared.
Why me? My little girl may not ever get to know her dad.
Why me?

Why was it me in the first place?

Sammi Waters (14)
Bentley Wood High School, Stanmore

WWII

I shot him - he tried to shoot me
That's the way it had to be
With a nine-inch pistol in my hand
I left him buried in the sand

Natural enemies him and I
Nazi and allies, that's what I mean
Good old allies won again
I feel sad now and then

I thought it would be an adventure
Joining the army - but I was wrong
I took a life - and that was bad
Now I'm feeling very sad!

Daniel Weir (13)
Bo'ness Academy, Bo'ness

Horse Riding

As I climb upon my horse, Starlight
I see his saddle shining bright
I urge him into a trot
I hope he doesn't see a fox

We start to get faster riding there
I feel the wind in my hair
The fields and hedges zooming past
Oh it's fun to go fast

I see a jump in my path
What do I do? I must think fast
We get closer to the hedge
I start to pull my horse's head

His legs come up and we soar over
I am so glad we landed in clover
As I jolt to a stop
I lean forwards and hug Starlight's throat

As we ride home now
We slow down to watch things go
We get back home and I get down
Oh, how I love riding along.

Hannah Speirs (13)
Bo'ness Academy, Bo'ness

What Are You Like?

Light that shines on hair so dark
As dark as brown tree bark

Eyes that twinkle like stars so bright
What cannot miss is out of sight

Bubbly and funny and pretty too
All are wonderful just like you!

Lauren Baillie (12)
Bo'ness Academy, Bo'ness

Football

Football is great
I like to play with my mate
I love scoring goals
I'm awesome and it shows

I play right wing
I cross it in
Before you know it
We win

I get frustrated
When I'm playing bad
And these feelings make me sad

At the end of the day
I'm just a child and so wild

Football's the best
Better than all the rest

The World Cup is coming up
I hope Spain will lift the cup.

Ross Monaghan (12)
Bo'ness Academy, Bo'ness

Number

I am a shining number
I glow in the dark
I shine in the park

Nothing to do
Just sitting there
Who else can I be?
Just a number

I am a small number to me
But I am a big number - people say!

What number am I?

Kelly Bissett (12)
Bo'ness Academy, Bo'ness

My Best Friend And I

My name is Amber
My best friend's Natasha
We both go to Bo'ness Academy
Our favourite subject is history

We walk each other to school each day
All Natasha talks about is her birthday
She will be 13 years old soon
And she is really over the moon

We call each other sisters
When she's on holiday I really miss her
She likes the same things as me
We dance to music as we hear it play
We listen to the same songs every day

When the music stops
So do we
We fall to the floor
In perfect harmony!

Amber Paterson (12)
Bo'ness Academy, Bo'ness

A Fly

So small, so fast, so fly,
You fly about the sky.
You sneak into houses,
You get frustrated with windows,
You never know the ways to go.
You fly about asking for trouble.
You buzz all day and buzz all night,
He just can't find you.
He stands there with his paper,
But you hide.
You hide with your pride.
So little fly, will you ever be found?

Courtney Wilson (13)
Bo'ness Academy, Bo'ness

Who Am I?

I am small,
But very tall,
Also loud,
But very proud.

I like going out and about.

My hair is brown,
I have a frown,

Who am I?

I have no brother,
But I have another,

I have a sister
Who is a pest.

Who am I?

You will never know,
I will just have to show.

Chloe Paterson (12)
Bo'ness Academy, Bo'ness

Bloom

A seed so small,
To a stock of green
Waiting to bloom
Into a beautiful scene.

Water, food and sunshine,
That's what it needs.
When raindrops hit
They lie there like beads.

A beautiful flower
That you once were,
But when I see you now
You're all grey, dull and bare.

Shanagh Penman (13)
Bo'ness Academy, Bo'ness

Oh, My Phone

It's hard as a bone
But it never leaves me alone
With its loud ringtone

Ring, ring it goes
But that only shows
That you should put it on silent

But the thing with silent
Is that it's very violent
When it vibrates in your pocket
So I'm going to lock it in a rocket
So that ringtone goes away
Into space, far away

Where there are aliens
Creatures and unknown
But I must admit it
I will miss my phone.

Matthew Cullen (12)
Bo'ness Academy, Bo'ness

Oliver Twist

Mist filled the air,
Not one moment could she spare.
Grabbing him tight and
Sneaking through the dark, eerie night.

Two people passed her.
Running, getting faster
Then suddenly she stopped.
She heard something hop.
Not far away stood he,
The one who is after thee.

Falling down flat, he hit her with a bat!
Dead was the beautiful Nancy!

Ellie Williams (12)
Bo'ness Academy, Bo'ness

Peter Crouch, The Couch

Crouch kicks the ball,
He is so tall.
His name is Crouch,
I thought it was Couch.
He likes to dance
And have a prance.
He heads the ball
Because he's 6ft tall
And all the rest are so small.
He played with Liverpool
But played like a fool
So he went to Portsmouth
And made the robot look cool.
So he moved to Spurs
And made Tottenham rule.
We hope you head England
All the way to the World Cup.

Jamie Argent (12)
Bo'ness Academy, Bo'ness

Boxer Puppy

So cute, so cuddly
In front of me there was a little boxer puppy
I didn't know what to call him
Boxer puppy, boxer puppy

My parents suggested that I call him Murphy
I decided to call him that
His little brown eyes sparkled every so brightly

As he plodded across the floor
I picked him up ever so carefully
I rocked him back and forth in my arms
His eyes started to shut ever so slightly
He fell asleep for the rest of the night
With his little brown teddy.

Lauren Stupart (12)
Bo'ness Academy, Bo'ness

Summer

Summer is the best time of the year
Listening to the kids shout and cheer
When they see the pool filling up
You see them smile and their faces light up

'Go and get the suncream on,' says Mum
We're thinking we don't need it on!

Now it's time to get in the pool
Shouting and screaming as it is cold.

Really I don't want to moan
I love the pool even though it is cold.

When summer leaves us
Autumn begins
We play in the leaves
But - everyone knows
Summer is the best season of all.

Joanna Bissett (12)
Bo'ness Academy, Bo'ness

The Wolf

At night his coat shines bright
His teeth glow in the moonlight
Beast by night, man by day
I wouldn't hunt it no matter how much you pay
He is the Devil's spawn, until comes dawn

The beast will howl
Hunters will scowl
They'll scream and shout
And when bitten will cry out
Even as it runs they call it runt

But I will not give up the hunt.

Connor Earle (12)
Bo'ness Academy, Bo'ness

My Dog, Kenzie

My dog, Kenzie, likes to play
He plays and plays every day
Well that's what I would like to say

But he doesn't
He lies down, doesn't frown
But you know when he sees your dinner plate
That is when he finds it great

He jumps and begs
He'll even stand up on his hind legs
But sometimes when I'm feeling great
I'll slip a little off my plate

Sometimes he will go into a frenzy
But he's still my dog, Kenzie.

Jordan Sharp (12)
Bo'ness Academy, Bo'ness

My Dad

My dad is tall and bold
As he strolls down the street
With his pure white
Nike trainers on his feet.

When in the house he lazes about,
Scott tiptoeing around
On his feet like a little mouse.
He likes TV and playing on his PS3
Whilst talking to me.

In his car he goes so fast
And I don't know if I'm going to last.

Outside school he tries to look cool
But I just see my dad looking like a fool!

Natasha Cameron (12)
Bo'ness Academy, Bo'ness

Murder

I saw this guy looking at me
I had to stab him - it had to be!
Now I'm standing in a corner, covered in blood.

He tried to cheat death
And so too did I
That's just the way he chose to die.

So I get back to my house
And there is no one there
When I go outside - I'm horrified to find
Police cars all around
The murderer's been found!

Matthew Martin (13)
Bo'ness Academy, Bo'ness

Designers

A designer has to concentrate
About which future stock to make
Necklines, cuffs and collars too
They must decide what to do.

What print, what design?
A skirt, a dress by Calvin Klein.

A designer has to set a price
So they can sell their merchandise.

Sunglasses, shoes and all
Designers try to get them in the shopping mall!

Laura Quigley (13)
Bo'ness Academy, Bo'ness

Tobi

Tobi when you were just a pup
You could fit into a tiny cup
It's sad when I hear you howling
When I shout at you for growling
When you jump up and down
As you look at me with those eyes so bright
What a lovely sight, so dark at night
Sometimes the stars are so bright
That they give me a fright
I love you with all my heart
As you have such a special bark.

Meghan Fraser (13)
Bo'ness Academy, Bo'ness

Computer Games

I like computer games
But it's quite a shame
I play them all day
And I must say
I'll end up like Mr Blobby
I need a new hobby!

I need to get out with my friends
All the time I could spend
Outside, playing all day
But I'll miss my Xbox, I must say.

Steven Graham (12)
Bo'ness Academy, Bo'ness

Hungry Owl

As night comes I awake
Ready to start my hunt
Flying through the air I search for some mice to eat
I search all night but I see no mice
My stomach growls as I fly
I see the sun about to rise
I fly back home with an empty tummy
As the sun begins to rise I'll fall asleep
Tomorrow will be another night
Look out mice! I'll be coming.

Hayley Calvert (12)
Bo'ness Academy, Bo'ness

Goodbye

Lauren shines like a star so bright,
Even in the dark moonlight.

When I was sitting looking at the sky,
I waved to her a farewell goodbye.

Rebecca Johnstone (12)
Bo'ness Academy, Bo'ness

Nature Dies But Stays Alive

When I see all the world I cry,
See all the flowers and trees die,
Nature is a beautiful thing that no one recognises until it's gone,
Right now, here is where you belong.
What would you do if you see the trees cut down?
When I say stop, they think I'm a clown.
Don't you see this is no game?
When you see the beauty gone, who will you blame?
So help now, together we can save the planet.
So now nature dies, but will stay alive.

Saleha Iftikhar (12)
Chadwell Heath Foundation School, Romford

69¢

69¢, remember your loved ones.
69¢, well it is affordable,
come to MESTEP's remember, remember for just 69¢.

So what do I get?
A cross, a plain white cross to symbolise my pain or theirs. The loss.
Just something pure white to resemble your being, your soul.
Remember your loved ones.

Endless boxes of fake flowers.
Empty cards waiting for messages to pass on.
Box number 1 TAB-18.
Plastic, cold, dead, pale imitations of life all for 69¢.

The door has the letters OUT in big capital letters.
Is it for those so encumbered by their grief that they need an exit?
A sanctuary from reality?
Into the light, OUT, but remember your loved ones.

Merry Christmas,
It's meant to be white and pure,
but look at me running from white crosses.
Look at me sitting in this diner.
Look at me.

You left, and here I am,
just filling that empty canvas with imitations of you,
look, you loved this horrible food, 18¢ a hot dog.
So I'll eat it for you, in your memory, not forgetting the extra chilli.
Jumbo size, bigger and better than ever.
So I eat, I eat, I eat and eat.

Merry Christmas everyone.
Just look at me here on this blessed day,
With my feast fit for a king, fit for you.
Another bite, swallow it, this fake respite,
Just bury it with food, mountains of it.
I want more, more.

69¢, 69¢, remember.
Remember your loved ones.
Remember, remember . . .

Zahrah Sheikh (18)
Chadwell Heath Foundation School, Romford

Sometimes It Happens

Happens an elderly life
Has lived off their life
And you can no longer help.
Happens that trouble may happen,
Horrid things happen,
Like thunder of Earth.
And . . .
Happens that strangest of things,
Craziest things,
Make you hate yourself . . .

But that's just a game . . .

Happens mysterious language,
Romantic language,
Can steal off your wealth.
Happens when a person tells you
They think just like you,
But they think not the same.
And . . .
Happens they look in your eyes,
Your genuine eyes,
And regret not a thing . . .

Happens that days can go by,
Slowly go by,
And it rots all your health.
Happens you think death's not there,
You think it's not there,
But it takes you at last.
Happens rarely, but happens,
A candle stops lighting,
A poison is gone . . .

Happens an elderly life
Has lived off the life
And won't be the same.
Happens that trouble my happen,
And when it can happen
They'll try and risk it.
Happens when mysterious language,

The known, well-old language,
Will never catch on.
And . . .

Happens rarely, but happens,
A candle stops lighting,
All life is all gone . . .

Migle Mickeveciute
Chadwell Heath Foundation School, Romford

Colours Of The Rainbow

Red
Red is the colour of fire,
Red is the colour of anger

Orange
Orange is bright,
Orange has a bubbly personality

Yellow
Yellow is the colour of pretty daffodils,
Yellow is the colour of the golden sand

Green
Green is the colour of the lush green grass,
Green is the colour of my favourite sweet

Blue
Blue is the colour of the calm sky,
Blue is the colour of the deep sea

Indigo
Indigo reminds me of royalty,
Indigo is the colour of my school uniform

Violet
Violet is the colour of my bed sheet,
Violet reminds me of a girly girl

Mix all these colours together,
You get a rainbow!

Hannah Puri (12)
Chadwell Heath Foundation School, Romford

Masking The Truth

Once again
She's deep in thought
Examining the encounter
And the feelings it brought

First came shock
And soon denial
You've inflicted pain
So now you smile

Acting oblivious
To what has occurred
To the wounds ripped open
And the apathy transferred

You stand before her
Smirking in success
You've broken her
She's emotionless

So now you see
That she truly cared
Though from your severity
She was not spared

So now she says
She has no interest
For her true thoughts
She cannot express

Another barrier
And more deceit
Being able to cry
Feels like a treat

The truth is masked
From your eyes
For though she smiles
Inside she cries.

Aisha Dowlut (13)
Chadwell Heath Foundation School, Romford

Thought Of Black

I asked him where you went
And when you were going to be back.
He looked at me. Then turned away,
Leaving me in thoughts of black.

I don't tell him I still remember your scent,
Sweet lavender and fresh grass.
I don't tell him I still cry when I see your photos,
He'd just get angry and shout, 'You can't undo the past!'

Daddy still hasn't told me where you are,
So I haven't deleted your number and still look out the door.
But now it's been one month, two months,
Am I not going to see you anymore?

I bottle up my tears, too many,
But now the bottle's not big enough.
Daddy doesn't understand it's killing me.
Sleepless nights, screams of fright, it's tough.

I miss you so much it's making me scream at 3am,
So Daddy's making me, again, see Eve.
I burn your photos to make me forget you
But you still remain, out of belief.

Eve says it's natural to think these things.
Shall I run away and do something to my wrist?
But I feel like a part of me is missing.
Eve says this is what happens with loss and miss.

I cover up my tears with a faint smile
And all those lies I try and fight.
Daddy asks, 'Are you OK, darling?'
'Yes, Daddy, yes I'm alright.'

I ask him where you went
And when you're going to be back.
However he still looks at me, still turns away,
Still leaves me in thoughts of black.

Reema Chandarana (12)
Chadwell Heath Foundation School, Romford

Down Behind The Dustbin
(Inspired by 'Down Behind the Dustbin' by Michael Rosen)

Down behind the dustbin
I met a dog called Mary
'What are you doing?' I said
'I'm playing with my fairy.'

Down behind the dustbin
I met a dog called Jack
'What are you doing?' I said
'I'm carrying my toy sack.'

Down behind the dustbin
I met a dog called Justin
'What are you doing?' I said
'I'm just dusting.'

Down behind the dustbin
I met a dog called Johnson
'What are you doing?' I said
'I'm just looking after my son, Thomson.'

Down behind the dustbin
I met a dog called Scruffy
'What are you doing?' I said
'I'm playing with my toy, Fluffy.'

Down behind the dustbin
I met a dog called Butter
'What are you doing?' I said
'I'm just cleaning up the clutter.'

Down behind the dustbin
I met a dog called Kent
'Do you own this bin?' I said
'No, I'm only the tenant.'

Mohammed Ruhel Amin (12)
Chadwell Heath Foundation School, Romford

Tinga
(Poem in the style of Beowulf)

Up,
Away from her castle
Through the shifting veil.
Over the plain of
Desolation,
Down to
The towers
Of
Jacaranda.

Over to the hall of rainbows.
The door was
Barred
And
Bolted.
The pale, white
Bony
Hand
Was placed on the door,
Pushing
Through the door.
With no trace of

Destruction

Creeping
Through the streets
Off she went
And
On she went.
Onwards lay her
Fate.

Samuel-Eliud Muturi (12)
Chadwell Heath Foundation School, Romford

Without Hope

My heart is like a song
That sings of only pain
Of all the things to remember
Only sadness remains

My only happy memories
Are being kept in a cell
Can I find happiness within
My self-inflicted hell?

My life is like a ghostly tree
With leaves left to die
My heart left to bleed
Can anyone save my life?

No one can tend to my shattered soul
It is smashed in too many places
Someone broke the path to my goal
And removed my place in life

My scars, my wounds
My nightmares, my grief
The stars and moons
They all turn on me

I'm as cold as ice
My heart's not beating at all
There's no life left in me
My heart has become as black as coal

What is hope?
What should I believe?
What is love?
Help me!

Rawdah Mahmood (12)
Chadwell Heath Foundation School, Romford

Manja
(Poem in the style of Beowulf)

He rose from his chair of success
Glanced around for something
This man
With pride and
No fear
Was the almighty
King Omis
As he looked around with his darting glare
Trying to locate
Him.

A poor peasant arrived
Urgent news
He purported, something's gone wrong
I saw the confusion on his face
Trying to understand
His pain
His anger
And sadness.

A late arrival it was
Naughty him
To every soldier and knight
He was an amateur
To the king he was not, however
Neither worthy.

What was he?

The son of Manja.

Nadia Patel (11)
Chadwell Heath Foundation School, Romford

Nyx
(Poem in the style of Beowulf)

Inky darkness
Engulfed the once placid scene.
Silence.
Violet, doe-like eyes twinkled
With ravenous hunger.
The blood-thirst
Man-foe
Travelled with a stealthy manner
To the grotty depot.
The deathly creature
Showed disapproval at
The filthy and grimy depot.
Closer and closer
He crept;
Alarm and dismay
Radiated from the depot.
Twisted strong hands clutched
Onto the door handle.
The door creaked open.
A putrid smell hit the creature's nostrils.
He clambered up the creaky stairs.
Briskly he made it to the summit
Of the stairs.
All of a sudden,
Violet eyes
Met
Jade-green eyes.

Sanjeet Dhinsa (12)
Chadwell Heath Foundation School, Romford

Tears Of Blood

Drip, drip, drip,
May the dagger of my peace
Remain in your heart.
The illusions of dreams
Will come alive one day.
Through death, life and time
You made me king.
You loved me for better, worse, rich or poor . . .
You gave me hope for every tear,
You were passionate as Cupid's arrow.
When you were gone
You returned to me in a heartbeat.
You were the treasure in my heart.

Fear, fear, fear,
Your simple touch faded away,
My blood-like tears drove down my body.
As I wept under the moonlight,
Longing for your faithful companionship.
I will never let you know how you broke my heart
And how it ripped me in two,
Under the luminous, lustrous moonlight.

You left me, betrayed my poor soul
And heart that's breaking in the distance.
Agony runs through my blood.
There is really only one thing left to say . . .
Revenge is interminable.

Navnit Dhaliwal (12)
Chadwell Heath Foundation School, Romford

Autumn Poem

Leaves are floating softly down,
Some are red, some are brown.
The wind goes swish through the air
And when you look back, there is no one there.

Chris Adebayo (12)
Chadwell Heath Foundation School, Romford

Masapius
(Poem in the style of Beowulf)

In the darkest hour of the winter night, Zipol
Came to Shalkon.
It had come here not once,
But twice,
But all the time
Up from its hidden lair,
Through the dirty slums,
And camouflaged with the mist.
Through the vigorous blizzard trudged
Zipol.
The Devil's-follower,
The death-lord,
It didn't shiver,
Not even once.
Zipol could smell the pure blood of Man
And was ready to take it.
The door was bolted.
Feeling humiliated,
In wrath
That any living being should even dare
To keep him out,
Zipol set the bloodthirsty,
Deadly devil-like hands
Against the door and

Burst in.

Amar Ladva (12)
Chadwell Heath Foundation School, Romford

Dowfow
(Poem in the style of Beowulf)

Dowfow always used to disguise into an
Amazing superhero
And then into an ordinary person.
Whenever he used to put on his costume
He felt a bit special and happy.
Dowfow enjoyed helping and
Saving people and doing
'His thing'!
Many people loved him
Deeply
And really wanted to find out his huge secret
About his
True identity.
The way he found out his missions
Was by using X-ray vision
And he was psychic.
He had a minute of thinking,
He could see that a young girl was about to be kidnapped.
As he stormed
Out the door, the girl's scream
Pierced his ears and made his
Heart beat
Extremely fast

But the only problem was . . .

Sadiyah Jaffar (12)
Chadwell Heath Foundation School, Romford

The Arrival-Way
(Poem in the style of Beowulf)

Manitol Cascaded
Through the castle,
Out of the woods,
Making his way home.
The thoughts Manitol had were simple,
Locate Bowser,
Find a sword,
A shield
And a suit of armour.
As he was walking, rain surged,
Minuscule drops of water poured
And quagmires were filled.
Manitol waded,
Strode
And promenaded
Through the deep
Muddy
And teeming quagmire.
Second by second,
Minute by minute,
Manitol was sinking in the mud
As if it were quicksand.
Manitol's feet were getting weak,
Weaker and weaker and weaker . . .

Rayan Shah (11)
Chadwell Heath Foundation School, Romford

The Expedition - Voyage
(Poem in the style of Beowulf)

King Pandon chose worthy warriors to assist Vica and Santez,
Covering the aqua liquid while the foe-person
Waited on the other side,
Soaring through the luxurious, gentle waves,
Crossing this way and that.
Relaxing on the water-traveller,
The sun beamed from deep within the sky
For night to arrive.
Gliding through the waves,
Hearing a disturbing thunderstorm,
A probable warning not to fight Banad,
Even then the journey carried on,
As time flew from dusk to dawn, swiftly
Sailing for Greenland.
When they were ready for the moment to come,
Journeying many sites, landscapes to discover,
Areas scorching like deserts,
Mystical rainforests,
Waterfalls leading into curious caves,
Mysterious animals travelling along the misty land.
Vica the Victorious made it to his destination.
Could this be the end for Vica?

Vinuri Vithanage (11)
Chadwell Heath Foundation School, Romford

Spooky

Sometimes I feel that life is spooky
When I put on the music that is groovy
And when I go to see a movie
I like to watch and eat a chewy
Sweet and also a chocolate cookie
Which melts in your mouth, so spooky
When I read at night.

Yanick Adjoumani (12)
Chadwell Heath Foundation School, Romford

Life-Changing
(Poem in the style of Beowulf)

When Picango told
These two people, Flosita and Goglo,
They were both so eager
And proud
To help the king.
From that moment their
Life-changing had commenced.
Swish, swash, as the waves
Violently crashed
Against the grey hazard.
The gloomy, miserable sky
Was filled with sky-shine.
As the sea-slicer
Travelled over the ripples
It slashed
Through the aggressive
Blue spikes. The sky-shine began to glisten
Even more upon the sea-slicer.
Flosita and Goglo had reached their final destination.
Once they got to land, in the corner of their eye
They spotted their
Wrath-giver's cave.

Simran Mahil (12)
Chadwell Heath Foundation School, Romford

Summer

Summer is my favourite time,
I love to watch the sun shine,
Happier than ever
I run around,
On the beach and through the sand,
As the sun shines through the grass,
I realise I have emptied my glass.

Summer Peters (12)
Chadwell Heath Foundation School, Romford

Singanta
(Poem in the style of Beowulf)

In the light of
The muted moon,
Bilmanki, the monster
Who sat in front of Ripturn Cave,
Who had heard about King Gritaria's mission for his men,
Strode on as the odium dispersed
Around his grisly, grotesque anatomy.
Bilmanki,
The death-bringer,
The man-killer.
As he advanced to the edge,
His eyes,
Red
Like living lava,
Scrutinised each inch of land
Lest they found Singanta.
Growling in vexation,
He cast his horrendous holocaust
On Singanta's ghostly boat
That drifted

In the translucent water.

Samaha Uddin (12)
Chadwell Heath Foundation School, Romford

Anger

When the toughness you show
Is the anger from below,
It's weakness that you decide
Whether to unveil or hide.

The spark of anger shines bright,
Belly of fire burns, alight.
Emotions decide which way to react,
Your heart must decide whether it's fiction or fact.

Emily Shah (11)
Chadwell Heath Foundation School, Romford

The Habitat-Shift
(Poem in the style of Beowulf)

The vision-helper scraped
Low in the sky.
Gugulion
Had to set off for his habitat-shift
Even though it was really early,
Because it would take hours to reach his destination,
His destiny
That was set by fate.
The sapphire liquid
Gleamed
At Gugulion.
Gugulion stepped into the wonderfully shaped
And crafted wave-cutter.
The boat dashed
And slashed
Through the sea.
Riding up
And down,
Then up and down cutting through
The sea.

Vithusan Jeevarajan (12)
Chadwell Heath Foundation School, Romford

Scream

There was a scream,
Then a light beam,
A door opened, bursting out was a lot of hot steam,
All that was left was a cone, no ice cream.
There was a stream,
There was a stream of more ice cream,
Coming down was a team,
A team of aliens, then I scream,
This has to be a dream.

Zainab Ahmed (12)
Chadwell Heath Foundation School, Romford

Meeting The Monster

In the darkest depth of day
Along the shadows crept Slythey, a cape of
Blackened light swamped him. Lone humans forced to fly in a
Single breath of his.
The scent of power poured out of him. Slythey
The death-prisoner,
Dungeon-raider.
Before long all people in the hall quivered in his presence
He was miles away.
He hovered along the muddy moors.
Lapping up fear as he walked through the hall wall
His bloodshot eyes fixed on his meal. Those eyes which,
If you stared through, would swallow you
Whole.
Those eyes to kill.
He slipped off a cape that was masking his face.
An aroma of deadly gas billowed out.
He decided his victim.
Emill.

Rachel Dinnes (11)
Chadwell Heath Foundation School, Romford

Fears The End Of Life

Doom is near
Because of fear
The end has come
Because of some
What's the cause?
It won't be fixed by Santa Claus
Maybe God just wants some blood
Why can't he take a flower bud?
Maybe if a certain child
Vowed their life to get the dead stars piled
You will find you need to be kind.

Bobby Curley (11)
Chadwell Heath Foundation School, Romford

Longing - Distance
(Poem in the style of Beowulf)

The boat shimmered
Across the fish-palace;
The boat was graceful as a bird.
It travelled the silky,
Watery waves to his destination.
While he travelled across the tranquil water
He gazed
Into the scorching horizon.
The sun sailed across the sky.
He was scared
To defeat Muschpuschsco,
But he was still brave.
He travelled for a while.
However
He finally found himself there.

His longing-distance
Surely had begun.

Jordan La Touche (11)
Chadwell Heath Foundation School, Romford

The Colour Purple

The colour purple is as delicate and deadly as it seems.
It's a swirling vortex through a deep, virtual world
Dominating everything else.
Performing jumps, twirls, swings and swirls,
Still deeply developing a life,
Focusing and defeating strife.
This is a life of an everlasting home run,
Running freely and dreamily.
Its unique qualities take it right from wrong,
Still staying strong.
This is rich, as precious as gold it can be,
This is the colour that leads.

Kumari Shyllon-Webb (11)
Chadwell Heath Foundation School, Romford

Broken Mirrors

Your love is like a broken mirror,
The one thing I thought was clear.

Your love is like a broken mirror,
Seven years of bad luck,
All my soul broken into pieces.

You're different in every reflection,
I can't recognise you,
You're a stranger to me.

I see your reflection,
But it's not you. It's your inner monster!
I finally see the real you.

The sharp corners cut me,
My blood dripping,
Just like my tears cried.

The shattered pieces of our love,
Thrown away like it meant nothing.

Anneka Patel (15)
Chadwell Heath Foundation School, Romford

Scream

I hear a scream,
I rush down and I see my brother is eating ice cream.
He says to go and get him cream.
I open the fridge and there is a light beam.
The kettle is on and the water is turning to steam.
Suddenly I'm in a football team.
Now I am in school, learning about the bloodstream.
My teacher always says, 'Don't daydream.'
My friend is asking me for a theme.
Now I am going home in a sunbeam.
I wake up by a bright gleam,
Then I notice it was all a dream.

Sharanga Thuvaraganathan (11)
Chadwell Heath Foundation School, Romford

Anger

Anger makes me feel sad
Anger makes me feel bad
Anger makes people cry
Anger makes people die
Anger wastes all your time
Anger makes you do crime
Anger is such a waste
Anger isn't a good taste!
Anger causes big wars
Anger closes our doors
Anger loses our friends
Anger breaks things, not mends
Anger brings us all down
Anger makes people frown
Anger ages your face
Anger just has no place!
Anger just isn't cool
Anger makes you a fool . . .

Francesca Burr (12)
Chadwell Heath Foundation School, Romford

The Love That Pours

You pour from the sky
On a miserable day.
Like tears fall from my eyes,
Until the pain begins to fade.

Sometimes rain is good,
Like the warm, gentle kind.
Or like a soulmate
With an open, loving mind.

Occasionally after the rain,
A rainbow will appear.
You'll be in their arms again,
And see the pain has disappeared.

Jade Wood (15)
Chadwell Heath Foundation School, Romford

Summer

A straw hat to shade my eyes,
As the morning sun starts to rise,
The sand crushes beneath my feet,
An ice cream sundae I have as a treat.
To soothe my burns from the sun,
I apply sunscreen one by one.
A game of beach volleyball I play,
I see the glistening sea softly sway.
The seagulls above me call,
I punch back the volleyball.
Mum shouts, 'The sun descends!'
I guess that's the call for my fun to end.
As I collect the forgotten shells
I stop and say my farewells
To the sun, sea and sand.
I pick up a little crab by its hand.
Through its rocky mouth I see it smile,
I put it down and watch it for a while.

Aliba Haque (12)
Chadwell Heath Foundation School, Romford

The Life-Path
(Poem in the style of Beowulf)

King Key Isi was shocked when he saw Mustabusta
But he still took him to the fish-path.
The fixation-fish went over the waves
Which were like crazing symbols
But did not make a sound.
Mustabusta knew his life-path would take hours,
Even days,
But Mustabusta was not scared.
Mustabusta was never scared.
As he travelled day and night,
Mustabusta was waiting for the moment
He saw the glimpse of the island.

Monique Reddock (12)
Chadwell Heath Foundation School, Romford

Old Man In A Cave

We found this old man living in a cave
To nature and elements he was a slave
Deep in the forest he hunted and trapped
Away from civilisation is where he was at
We told him it was time for him to go
Back with us to society, but he said, 'No
I will not go to your cars, TV and electricity'
That's when we knew he had lost his sanity
Old as dirt, living for years off the land
No lights, store or even a name brand
We insisted, 'There are places for folks like you
A happy place, with others and lots to do!'
He protested, struggled and gave a fuss
I gave him a pill and he went with us
Took him to the ward and I heard he's sick
We did our part, now he may not make it
Thanks to us at least he was able to see all this
For one brief moment, he got to share our bliss.

Haroon Ikram (15)
Chadwell Heath Foundation School, Romford

The Unwanted Owl In Me

Always there on your own,
You're never visible,
But you always make noise.
Always there at night,
Making the noises in my head.
Always there at the cemetery,
Telling me I might end there.
Fortunately you do go away,
But you also come back, uninvited and unwanted.

Prabhjit Singh (15)
Chadwell Heath Foundation School, Romford

How My School Day Begins!

It's Monday morning at 7.01
I'm still half-asleep, my homework's half-done
My shower is cold, my Weetabix is dry.
My mother forgets to kiss me goodbye.

I'm walking to school
It's thirty degrees
My fingers won't work
My toes and ears freeze . . .

I slip on school steps
I trip in the hall
The toilet floods in the bathroom stall
The gym door is locked; library the same
The head teacher greets me with the wrong name.

Finally I'm in the classroom
It's 8.01, it's Monday morning
My school day has just begun.

Saira Arshad (11)
Chadwell Heath Foundation School, Romford

The Fish-Home

'Fri, Fri, time to go, your ship awaits you.'
Fri did not wake
But finally he woke and off he went.
As he waved goodbye,
He then told himself,
'I have got to kill this monster.'
A storm ahead, Fri did not see the storm,
He sailed right into the storm.
'Help!' he yelled.
He thought, *must keep going, no turning back.*
He carried on and
Finally he reached land and slept in the boat
When the sky-light was at its brightest.

Ross Dipple (11)
Chadwell Heath Foundation School, Romford

Pain

Pain is the constant falling rain,
The same that glooms right over your brain.
Someone close to you got shot
And blood is dripping down the drain.
Someone being whipped by a cane,
It drives me insane.
My energy is gone I feel emotionless.
Being hit by a blow dart,
It's like your brother being blown apart.
It's not just a toothache,
It's a heartbreak.
When the teardrops fall from my eyes,
Like when someone close to you dies,
Your relatives just cry and cry.
When your heart has just torn,
It's not a bad thing to wish you weren't born.

Michael Jordan (11)
Chadwell Heath Foundation School, Romford

The Writer Of This Poem
(Based on 'The Writer of This Poem' by Roger McGough)

The writer of this poem is smart
And has a very, very big heart.
As sly as a fox,
And has never had chickenpox.

The writer of this poem is as tall as a door
And as slim as a claw.
As cool as the wind
And as fresh as a mint.

The writer of this poem is as clever as a tick
And as sharp as a tip.
As delicate as a flower
And is one in a million
(At least that's what the poem says!)

Navreet Dhaliwal (12)
Chadwell Heath Foundation School, Romford

Past Poets - Future Voices Visions Of Youth

Purple Peace

The colour purple is the love between a mother and her child.
The purple love lights up the nights like fireworks
on Bonfire Night.
When you see purple, the area turns crime-free.
No one likes anger; anger scars you for life like a weapon
called a knife.
Purple is peace,
Peace makes you calm,
Peace feels like you're holding a dove in your palm.
Purple is the symbol for love and peace,
But is purple a colour that can change from magnificent
like the sunset
To mysterious like the darkest corner in your room?
Purple!
Who knows . . . ?

Naveed Ur Rahman (12)
Chadwell Heath Foundation School, Romford

The Journey

Shinflet set off on his
Time-taken journey,
Dragging his gleaming sword behind him.
He strolled for hours
Under the heat-devil.
He dropped to
The cracked ground
To rest.
He gazed up and saw little bolts of light
Then he slowly fell to sleep.
The next morning he woke thirsty
And saw hallucinations.
He staggered another mile or two.
In his sight he saw
The deep, dark valley.

Chlöe Brown (12)
Chadwell Heath Foundation School, Romford

Gadaro
(Poem in the style of Beowulf)

The powerful, muscular man
Entering the dilapidated country, Supaurse.
A man called him and said, 'Your name?'
The muscular man answered, 'Gadaro.'
The strange man said, 'Oh Gadaro, King Rayed awaits you.'
He went to see King Rayed.
When he got there he saw the king covered in rubies and gems.

King Rayed said, 'Gadaro, are you well known to your people?'
Gadaro answered, 'Yes, they trust me and have faith in me.'
'Gadaro, we need your help.
We have a red-eyed, black dagger monster.
His name is Ganit!

Will you please help us . . . ?'

Noreen Pokun (12)
Chadwell Heath Foundation School, Romford

Ghost

I had a dream about a ghost
Who was as dumb as a post
Eating chicken roast
He likes the host
By Ivory Coast
He is also a boast
And he loves buttered toast
And he talks the most
The next day
I heard a scream
That was mean
While eating ice cream
And it had a bad theme
Then I saw a beam.

Kori Meikle (12)
Chadwell Heath Foundation School, Romford

Past Poets - Future Voices Visions Of Youth

Love

Love is something you look forward to,
Not someone who lets you down
And who you knew.
He broke my heart again and again,
With sorrow and grief, what did he gain?
All the happiness drained from me,
Love is something he once gave to me!
Day by day nothing is left,
All the tears I cry and now I'm dead.

Aliza Alam (13)
Chadwell Heath Foundation School, Romford

Ghost

I once saw a ghost,
Who was as dumb as a post,
So I went to the kitchen and made him some toast.
He said we could share it, but he ate the most,
I showed him my medals but he said not to boast.
He said he was still hungry so I cooked him a roast.
We acted out a TV quiz and he was the host.

Nicole Johnson (12)
Chadwell Heath Foundation School, Romford

Teenagers

Teenagers, they are all the same
Every day after school
Every weekend, time to be free
No teenager wants to be caged
All we want is to run free
Going places with our friends
Spending every second as ourselves
Running free like the wind
Spreading our wings once again.

Charlene Hardy (14)
Dunluce School, Bushmills

The Break Of Dawn

The break of dawn
Is almost here,
The break of dawn
Is oh so near.

I'm in my trench
Wanting to sleep,
Water everywhere
Drowning my feet.

Every day,
Every morning,
Bombs go off
With no warning.

All I hear are
Shell bombs screaming,
Young men scared
Just sitting and weeping.

Don't want to wake,
Please let me go home,
So many soldiers, but yet
I feel so alone.

Morning now here,
I can see the sun,
Must get myself up,
Must grab my gun.

My mother's voice
I long to hear,
The break of dawn
Is oh so near.

Anna Thompson (14)
Dunluce School, Bushmills

We Don't Know Who We Are

I'm a person
Just a normal person
Yet classed as a teenager
Becoming one
Changes everything
The world, always against you
Weight on our shoulders
We need to lift
The weight and be strong
Why do we change?
For others?
To suit them?
We're ourselves
Still the same
We act different
We're young
Yet growing older each day
People never seem happy
Why is it so wrong
For us to have fun
Friends or even family?
Ashamed of us
Ashamed of ourselves
Often hiding
Sometimes climbing
Yes
Nothing ever seems right
Have more trust in us!
Trust in ourselves!
They call me a teenager.

Abbie Harte (14)
Dunluce School, Bushmills

The Vinegar Incident

My tenth birthday,
I went looking for my dad.
I tiptoed to the kitchen to scare him,
But found not him . . .
But food spread.

There were cocktail sausages,
Buns, sweets, mini pizzas,
In colourful plates and dishes.
With balloon-covered cups,
Filled with fizzing, sparkling drinks.

Not forgetting the thick, sweet, pink iced cake.

I saw what I thought was a drink that I wasn't allowed.
I grabbed it
And ran . . .

I sat in the corner of my room
And it drizzled down the back of my throat.
My eyes watering, lips turning with the bitterness,
And my nose tickled with the sour smell.

It was disgusting and sour,
I couldn't believe it -

I had drunk half a bottle of vinegar.

Kyra McLaughlin (14)
Dunluce School, Bushmills

The Old Door

The old wooden door,
Eaten and broken,
Creaks and cracks open
With a mouth like a lion,
Till the old door
Takes no more . . .
It falls and smashes.

Ellen Devenney (13)
Dunluce School, Bushmills

I Am Who I Am

I am who I am,
And that's who I will be.
I wish everybody would see who I am,
Let me be free.

Never getting my own point of view,
Always trying to skip the queue,
I wish I could just let go,
I feel like running away from home.

Parents always shouting,
'You did this!'
You did that!'
As if they would know.

I feel like smiling,
I feel like crying,
I just want a hug,
I'll be fine.

All you need to know is
I am who I am,
No one can change that -
That will be me.

Jessica Harris (14)
Dunluce School, Bushmills

The Lion

As the lion creeps through
The safari grasses
It crawls as quiet
As a flower bud sprouting
He takes a whiff
To sniff out his prey.

He took a pounce
And there he lay.

Arianne Stirling (12)
Dunluce School, Bushmills

The Roller Coaster

As I climb the old battered tin stairs,
There it is . . .
The brand new roller coaster ready to go.
All is silent until I sit down.
Children come running and stomping,
All is not silent anymore.
A loud horn is heard and then a hiss,
And off we go around the track.
Clunk, up the hill.
Clunk, clunk, clunk
Along the top,
Clickity-clack.
Up and down.
Clickity-clack.
Here we go down the hill,
Children and adults screaming loud.
Around a loop and the bend,
Now it's over,
We come to a halt.
That was fun,
I'll go again!

David Fillis (13)
Dunluce School, Bushmills

How To Make A Monster

It needs:

A face like a shovel
Built like a fish tank
Eyes like flames
A belly the size of a truck
A nose like a pig
Hair like Mount Everest
A tail like a snake
Teeth like spears.

Kyle McLelland (12)
Dunluce School, Bushmills

Dreams Unknown

When I was younger
I knew who to be
But now I'm a teen I can't see.

I walk out the door
Heart on my sleeve
Thinking of people
I aspire to be.

My father says
I should know by now
But truth be told
I'm just a child.

I weigh out my options
Hopes and dreams
I picture my life
In so many scenes.

The scene I choose
Will be my own
Because I am a teen
Dreams unknown.

Sara Dallat (14)
Dunluce School, Bushmills

My Big Monster

It needs:
A head like a big round balloon
A body like a big building
Ears like big sheets flapping in the wind
Teeth like small, sharp pencil leads
Eyes like great big footballs
A voice like a washing machine on full
Arms like skinny twigs
Fur like ripped carpets all patched up
A tail like a long eel.

Chelsea O'Doherty (12)
Dunluce School, Bushmills

The Bully Or The Bullied?

It is going to happen.
Big Charlie Bruce is going to beat me up
For the third time, in one hour.
The hour passes,
It is break.
Charlie walks up to me,
Mr Nichol walks by.
Big Charlie Bruce gives me a hug,
Hits me a thud,
I fall in the mud.

It is going to happen.
I am going to beat up wee Charlie Bruce
For the third time, in one hour.
One hour passes
It is break.
Mr Nichol walks by.
I give wee Charlie Bruce a hug,
Hit him a thud,
He falls in the mud.

Jordan Ramage (14)
Dunluce School, Bushmills

Clocks

The clicking clock goes *tick-tock,*
Tick-tock, day in and day out.
A talky clock would go talk-talk
And tell me everything.
A noisy clock would go *ring-ring*
And would wake the house up.
A quiet clock would be
Quiet as a mouse.
There are lots of different clocks
Around the world and yet they all go
Tick-tock.

Kelly McKissick (13)
Dunluce School, Bushmills

Can't Think Of Anything To Write

I'm sitting here in the computer suite
With a blank page in front of me.
I don't know what to write,
I might as well go on a shopping spree.
OK, that didn't make much sense
But hey, I can't think of anything to write.

I'm sitting here in the computer suite
With six lines of writing in front of me.
I still don't know what to write.
Does this look alright?

My poem is really short,
Don't give me a report,
It's not my fault I can't rhyme,
Don't tell me this is a crime.

I'm sitting here on this rhyming site
Still thinking of what to write.

Catherine Duclayan (14)
Dunluce School, Bushmills

Island Of Lost Dreams!

On this extreme island,
Dreams are far from hands' reach,
Lying on a white and sandy beach,
Nothing to think about and dream,
Feeling the Atlantic sea beam.

Night soon comes around,
What to dream becomes a blur,
Neither picture nor sound,
As I look around for something to dream,
Pictures and words are lost in my mind.

On this extreme island,
Dreams are far from hands' reach.

Cathy Hogg (14)
Dunluce School, Bushmills

How To Make A Monster?

It needs:

A head like a pointy ice cream cone,
A body like a large balloon, shiny and round,
Eyes like large footballs,
Ears like horns, big and long,
Teeth like sharp knives,
Whiskers like long strips of paper,
A voice like a frog on a lily pad,
Skin like rough sandpaper,
A tail like the body of a snake,
A tongue like burning flames of fire,
A mouth like a loud whistle,
Arms like long tree trunks,
Legs like a very long pole.

Rebecca Knowles (12)
Dunluce School, Bushmills

Inner City Life

Every day walking down the street,
Thinking of who I'm going to meet.
In my bag I've got a piece of meat
Between two buns,
Should I eat?

There's two bums on the street
Eyeing me up like I'm a treat.
One walks up to me with his smelly feet,
Not to greet or to meet.

Looks like trouble outside the bubble,
He talks to me in a struggle,
All drugged-up like he's been mugged.

Inner city life, inner city pressure.

Joshua McCartney (14)
Dunluce School, Bushmills

Why Me?

Who said love was easy?

We said we would be forever,
I thought you meant it!

I would risk my life for you,
I thought you felt the same way,
Obviously not.

I never really fell in love with you.

Between all the laughter,
All the memories we had together,
But I guess I just fell in love
With our friendship.

Chloe Freeman & Sophie Keys (14)
Dunluce School, Bushmills

Teenager

T for trustworthy
E for enthusiastic
E for easygoing
N for normal
A for ambitious
G for goodwill
E for energetic
R for reliable

Teenagers - old enough to
Control their own lives.
Why can't adults get this
Into their minds?

Brent Smith (14)
Dunluce School, Bushmills

The Pet Shop

The pet shop with a cat that roared like a lion.
A dog that crunched on a big old bone, *crunch*.
Then *munch, munch*
From a bird that sat on a branch.
And *vroom, vroom, vroom*
From hamsters running on the floor.
Grinding on the noisy floor with a colony of ants
Skittering and scattering,
Up, down and all around,
Annoying the bats with their infernal scream,
In the back storeroom
It's a jungle and so much more . . .

Luke Philpott (13)
Dunluce School, Bushmills

Teenagers

Teenage life is a hard life
When you've got nothing to do.
We have ups and downs,
People acting like clowns,
They don't have a clue!

They fight on the streets,
Try to avoid the police,
Some just can't get free.

I'd love one day
For it all to be OK,
But I guess that's another day!

Amy O'Brien (14)
Dunluce School, Bushmills

Concert

The buzzing and bashing of the loud
Music banging.

The clapping and the clashing of the crowd
Of people cheering.

The ding and the dong of the rhythm
Of the song.

The screeching and the scratching of
The high-pitched guitar.

The batter and the clatter of the floor
About to shatter.

Alex O'Neill (13)
Dunluce School, Bushmills

In The Dark

Alone in the dark.

No one around me,
Beside me,
Nor in front.

In the dark,
Kept in the dark.

There is no one.

Just me, all by
Myself
In the dark.

Abbie Dunlop (14)
Dunluce School, Bushmills

How To Make A Monster

It needs:
A head as round as a clock,
A voice like a washing machine turned on full wash,
Body as wide as a double-decker bus,
Fur like ripped curtains, one on top of another,
A nose as long and pointy as Big Ben,
Paws like balloons with no air, flat and round,
Eyes like two bulging keyholes,
Legs like broomsticks, thin and rough,
A tongue like an old carpet, rough and dirty,
Teeth like bits of bamboo, brown and long.

Stefanie Patton (12)
Dunluce School, Bushmills

How To Make A Monster

A body like a tree
A head like a laptop
Teeth like bullets
Arms like a snake
Legs like a shovel
Feet like bikes
Hands like books
Eyes like balloons
A nose like a piano
A mouth like a keyboard
Hair like a brush.

Aaron Agnew (12)
Dunluce School, Bushmills

My Dragon

A nose as sharp as a dagger
A head like a sieve
A body like a grandfather clock
Eyes like sparkling diamonds
Teeth like sparkling icicles
Whiskers like knitting wool
A tongue like a snake's body
Legs like a mouse's tail
Scales like flakes of gold
A voice like two lions, a cat
And a dog fighting.

Johnathan McGowan (12)
Dunluce School, Bushmills

My Cool Dragon

A nose like a hard conker,
A head like an oddly-shaped house,
A body like a long train track,
Eyes like piercing diamonds,
Teeth like a shiny, fresh-cleaned car,
Whiskers like long knitting needles,
A tongue like red cherries,
Legs like bulldozers,
Scales like flakes of gold,
A voice like a tractor crashing.

Billy Grant (12)
Dunluce School, Bushmills

How To Make A Monster

Body like a bomb
Head like a plane
Teeth like bullets
Arms like Big Ben
Legs like the Empire State Building
Tail like a propeller
Mouth like a razor
Nose like a lemon
Eyes like hot air balloons
Ears like satellite dishes.

David Kelly (11)
Dunluce School, Bushmills

The Clingy Crab

Swimming in a pool with an unknown crab,
I suddenly feel an almighty grab.
I jump without joy, scream and shout,
It's stuck to my toe like a big red bow!
It will not budge, as if it has some sort of grudge!
The skitter won't move and I'm making a groove!
It keeps on biting and I keep on fighting.
The claws are so sharp that they're leaving a mark!
It suddenly lets go, but it is now my toe
That looks like a big red bow!

Tanith Speers (14)
Dunluce School, Bushmills

The Storm

Crash, bang, splash, roared the waves.
Ping, pong, plop, hit the rain.
Crash, clang, clatter, bangs the rain on the garage door.
Swiftly, smoothly goes the wind
Gently moving along the street.

Matthew Nicholl (13)
Dunluce School, Bushmills

My Dragon

A head like an ice cream cone,
A mouth like a large caravan,
Teeth like sharp kitchen knives,
A tail like a slithering snake, wet and smooth,
Voice like a roaring lion strong and loud,
Legs like large walking sticks,
A body like glowing lights,
Eyes like fresh green apples,
Arms like large tree trunks,
Whiskers like large strips of paper.

Brad Moore (12)
Dunluce School, Bushmills

Swimming Pool Fun

The children splashing and sploshing
While they scream and screech.
The beach balls smack the water
And shower and sprinkle
The children's faces.
Children choke on the water
While adults are
Sleeping
    Softly
        On their seats.

Jack Milligan (12)
Dunluce School, Bushmills

My Monster

A nose like a balloon, big and round
A mouth like a football, squashed and flat
Eyes like rugby balls with blood on them
Ears like a bow and arrow, pointy and sharp
Tails like snakes', long and skinny
Claws like needles, spiky and small
Fingers like knives, silver and lethal
Fur as smelly as mud
Scales like sandpaper, rough and dirty
Paws like nails, sharp and long.

Bradley Barber (12)
Dunluce School, Bushmills

My Dragon

A head the shape of the Eiffel Tower,
A body like a tank, wide and long,
Ears like a honk from far away,
A mouth like a vampire, covered in blood,
Teeth as sharp as a razor,
Eyes like an eagle, long and sharp,
Legs like a kangaroo bouncing in the air,
Claws like a crocodile's, long and sharp,
Tail like a snake, slippery and long,
Arms like an elephant, big and fat.

Christopher Macauley (12)
Dunluce School, Bushmills

A Monster Poem!

Teeth as black as coal,
A nasty, scary snout.
Hair as long as sticks
And nails like toothpicks.
A body the size of a king-size bed
And feet like mighty monster trucks.
Eyes as red as devils' blood
And muscles as hard as metal studs.
Ears as big as saucepan lids
And a mighty roar like a foghorn!

Owen Black (12)
Dunluce School, Bushmills

Teenagers

T eenagers, we have it so hard
E xams are a bother, so troublesome too
E xcuses for PE. 'What's wrong with you?'
'N onsense! There's no such word as can't, the teachers shout!
A cting out, time to rebel; is that what this is all about?
G CSEs soon, need to revise. Why, Mr Bee? Why we?
E ccentric students, so different from me
R ainy days, have to trek to school
S ummer is much too long away, can't wait,
    Please, oh please Mum, can't I stay at home with you?

Nicole Brown (14)
Dunluce School, Bushmills

Monster

A head like an apple, shiny and red
A body like a tank, wide and strong
Wings like a dragon
Snout like a cat, fat and pink
Tail like a snake, scales slithery out of the water
Talons like an eagle's, sharp and broad
Fangs like bats', bursting for blood
Sails like a lizard jumping around
Ears like a rabbit eating a carrot
Voice like a dog panting away.

Craig Nelson (12)
Dunluce School, Bushmills

How To Make A Baby Elephant

It needs:
A head the shape of an oval
A trunk as long as a giant lollipop stick
Ears the shape of half a heart
Eyes the size of a fingernail
A body like a big rectangle
Legs as thick as a brick
A tail as light as a feather.

Melissa Duncan (12)
Dunluce School, Bushmills

The School Bus

The screaming
The shouting
The footsteps hitting
Off the metal steps.

The banging of all the lunch boxes
Being bounced off the floor.

Lauren Williamson (13)
Dunluce School, Bushmills

Little Leaves . . .

Little brown leaves
Rustling up the footpath
Crunching and scrunching
Along the doorsteps
Blowing and flowing
In the evening breeze
The little brown leaves
Are out to please.

Melissa Rainey (13)
Dunluce School, Bushmills

My Stream

The swirling stream going over
The rocks, going past
Me and into the sea.
It keeps on
Flowing and flowing
Down
The mountain top
Like a squish-squash mop.

Regan White (13)
Dunluce School, Bushmills

How To Make An Edible Monster

It needs:
A head as flat as a pancake,
A body as wobbly as jelly,
Eyes like bonbons,
Arms like lollipops,
Hair like spaghetti,
A nose like a jelly baby,
Legs as slippery as butter.

Bethany Hannah (12)
Dunluce School, Bushmills

The Hall

In the hall children were laughing,
When the headmaster came along,
The laughing stopped.
When he talked they were quiet,
All of a sudden they started a riot.
To detention they all went, with the work they were given.
They were put out of detention,
Then they were back to normal again.

Steven Lyons (13)
Dunluce School, Bushmills

It Makes Sense

Happiness is like the blue sky above you
Happiness tastes as sweet as sugar
It smells like melting chocolate
And looks like flowers on a summer's day
Happiness sounds like birds tweeting in a tree
And feels as smooth as silk.

Dylan McKendry (12)
Dunluce School, Bushmills

The School Bell

Ding-a-ling-ling, goes the school bell
The children crashing and bashing
To be the first to tell
That school went well
Buses and cars queuing to go home and
Thank you for listening to my lovely poem.

Jamie McKee (13)
Dunluce School, Bushmills

Shoes

Clip, clop, clip, clop,
Time to go to the shop
Looking for shoes.
Pink ones, blue ones and yellow ones too,
What colour should I buy?
Mum, give us a clue!

Hannah McClarty (12)
Dunluce School, Bushmills

At The Beach

Children splishing and splashing in the water
Clashing off the waves
Eating their ice creams
Sitting in the sand
Acting like animals
Playing in the caves.

Ben Walker (13)
Dunluce School, Bushmills

ET

ET must go home right now
He wants to go home soon
He would like to phone home
And he looks like a baboon

Elliott must help him now
ET is rather lost
He should go back to his planet
ET escapes at a high cost

Elliott's bike can fly
With ET in the basket
To lose the government
ET tries to mask it.

Kane West (13)
St Peter's School, Bournemouth

Mother, What Have You Done?

He's just a lonely child
Crying in his cot
Waiting for his mother to save him
Waiting for the love he never got

She's just an innocent girl
With no one there to help
Her brother is crying again
But she cannot calm his yelp

She moves along the landing
Heart thudding in her chest
Edging towards her brother's room
To stop him being a pest

She dares not breathe
For fear her mother shall hear
Treading carefully step by step
Until his room is near

She smells the foul alcohol
She smells the vile drug
Her mother's been at it again
While she'd been tucked up in her bed all snug

She is closer to his room
A smile spreads on her face
But something is not right
Something is out of place

She enters the room with caution
Her brother's breath is gone
His tiny little body is still
His short-lived life is done

The girl sinks to the ground
She cannot make a noise
Her little brother is dead
She's unable to keep her poise

Past Poets - Future Voices Visions Of Youth

Her mother bangs open the door
'What did you do?' she screams
But the girl cannot move, her eyes are full
Her mother cares not it seems

'You killed him!' she yells
Her eyes bloodshot and crazy
The girl is frightened, a thousand tears fall
Soon she shall be pushing her daisy

The poor girl stays
She holds her brother's corpse
Her mother returns, broken bottle in hand
The boy's deathly face gawps

Her mother lunges
The girl's tears still do fall
She does not want to live without him
Her mother drags her, by her hair, to the hall

The girl does not move
Just clutches her brother tight
Her mother takes the bottle
And stabs with all her might

Mother, what have you done?
Both your children are dead
The girl's blood drips scarlet on your hands
Is something wrong with your head?

Mother, what are you doing?
Hunting something down?
Looking for something in particular
To ease your demented crown?

Is that what I think it is?
Is that ecstasy you're taking?
To feed that hungry habit of yours
That you were so close to breaking?

What is that you're doing?
You've poured them all into your hand
Don't tell me overdose is the way
You want to leave this land

Tears stream down your face
Are you starting to feel regret
For killing your innocent daughter
And leaving your son to cry, don't forget?

One, two, three, up goes your hand to your mouth
Your brain is telling you that this action is bad
What a way to end your life
It really is quite sad

Ten minutes and it's complete
Your time is very near
You crawl towards your dead children
And as you die by their sides, you shed a single tear

Next morning the news is all around the quiet house
Neighbours heard the shouts and called the cops
They saw you three huddled together
Finally your family's screaming stops

There is one thing you forgot, dear mother,
One rather big thing I must state before I part
The bloody bottle in your hand
The stab wound through your daughter's heart

The pills rammed down your throat
The drugs all over the floor
The smell of the alcohol and pills
That strikes as you walk through the door

If you were alive, Mother
You would stand trial for murder
But seeing as you took your life
You need to look no further

Mother, Janie and Elliot
You all left this world together
In the space of forty minutes
Now you shall spend eternity with each other, forever

Past Poets - Future Voices Visions Of Youth

Dear reader
I'm sorry to have taken up your time
With such a tale of horror
But whenever you feel like you've had a rough day
Think of Janie and Elliot's terror

Look at this poem
Then you will see
Your life isn't as bad
As you make it out to be.

Olivia Arnaudy (13)
St Peter's School, Bournemouth

The Box

There we were,
All gathered around.
Telling our stories,
Not making a sound.

Then this one girl came up to us all,
She sat down and started to tell
The story of her life,
Which seemed to dwell.

She told us about her disasters,
She told us where she was sent.
She told us about those happy days,
And this is how it went:

'When I was four, my mother left me,
One day she just wasn't there.
It was strange with her not around,
I always wonder where?

What did I do wrong?
Why did she leave me?
Was it his fault?
Or was it caused by me?

As I grew older, I never forgot,
About all those happy days
I spent with my mother,
All those happy plays.

At the age of twelve I started to wonder,
What really happened that night.
When I never saw my mother again,
Did she really catch that flight?

I started to dream of all the possibilities,
Of where my mother could be.
I dreamed that one day she would return,
Return home for me.

When my father was out,
I went into the loft.
It was out of bounds for me,

Past Poets - Future Voices Visions Of Youth

And it had a strange waft.

It felt like someone was there,
Someone watching me.
It was cold and I was scared,
But who could it be?

I sat in the loft,
With my head in the clouds.
Wondering what was to hide,
Why it was out of bounds.

But out the corner of my eye,
I noticed a box.
It felt like I was meant to find it,
Like prey to die for a fox.

I opened the box slowly with care,
Thinking of what could be inside.
It is probably nothing, I thought to myself,
But maybe this is what was to hide.

Inside the box were old pictures,
Memories of someone maybe.
A diary and some hair,
A girl could it be?

I then saw a certificate,
Kim Thomas it had.
I was hoping I was wrong,
But I was thinking something bad.

Maybe that is why I never saw my mother again,
She had died and passed away.
I thought of all our happy memories,
And all the days we did play.

But there was something else in the box,
A letter, all old and torn.
It had tea stains on it,
And it looked very worn.

On the front it had my name,
Was it for me?
I started to open it slowly,
Not knowing what it could be.

Was it from my mum?
Why had I not seen it?
I wondered what it contained,
Should I really read it?

The letter really spoke to me,
As if my mum was there.
It told me where she had been,
And why she was never there.

She loved me very dearly,
And wrote this when she was ill.
It told me how sorry she was,
And why she was about to take the pill.

She was too sick.
And could not take the pain anymore,
She never thought it would end that way,
And that is when she fell to the floor.

It made me cry and wonder,
What life would be like if she was here.
Everything made sense now,
It all became so clear.

I heard my dad come home,
And ran with the letter to him.
I asked why he had not told me
About my dear mother, Kim.

He looked at the letter,
Crying as he read.
He remembered what had happened,
And what came back in his head.

We sat there together,
Looking very grim.
Remembering all the good things,
About my dear mother, Kim.

Past Poets - Future Voices Visions Of Youth

I still remember her now,
All the things we did.
I am glad I found that box,
Though it was well hid.'

Zoe Mundell (13)
St Peter's School, Bournemouth

The Irreplaceable

Love and family
Smiles, hugs and kisses
All the children together
Praying for their hopes and wishes

As the days went by
Sadness came, no joy
Everyone was so sad and still
That not even a baby played with his toy

Why did it happen to them?
They blame themselves
As they make their way to the church
Following the chimes of the church bells

No one to hold when I'm feeling sad
No one standing there to see
No one left to give the right answer
No one left for me

My eyes start to water
I try hard to be brave
How can I do this
When my mother's not there to save?

We were so close
My mother and I
What could have happened?
How did she die?

Annabelle Buckfield (13)
St Peter's School, Bournemouth

Memoirs

I have a friend who used to live,
But under earth does lie,
For on that foggy morning,
My friend, my friend did die.

Walking along, quite happily,
Whis'ling a carefree tune,
Past a sinister sentry,
'Neath the carefree moon.

We were together, him and I,
No happier pair than we,
But that friendship that we treasured
Did end so suddenly.

A thousand sparks make a lightning bolt,
That, anyone does know,
But a thousand thousand tiny sparks
Does fill one's heart with woe.

Lit up was the whole night sky,
And under it we trembled,
The light so bright it hurt to see,
The Earth itself did tremble

As a thousand thousand angels
Did clap at such a sight,
And the sound that filled the still night air
Was victory and might.

The heavens opened then it came,
A torrential downpour,
Yet still we hadn't seen it all
What the night had set in store.

They came in marching, row on row,
In our stupor we stared,
Advancing slowly, ever nearer,
With menacing eyes they glared.

Past Poets - Future Voices Visions Of Youth

Thudding footsteps, louder now,
Twiggy limbs, bushy hair,
Formation slowed, halting now,
They met our frightened stare.

There we stood, unable to move,
Speechless, petrified,
Surrounded, hemmed in on every side,
We would not make it out alive.

The forest stood before us now,
The spirit world we entered,
Filled with fantasy galore,
About us it was centred.

I heard a scream, a piercing shriek,
And then another spoke;
'Calm yourself, we mean no harm,'
It was the mighty oak.

'Will you stand with us?
Fight by our side?
No, for we will suffer greatly,
You will wish to hide.'

But Trevor was ever contrary,
And he did wish to fight,
Outside, the wall of saplings,
They gleamed in early light.

Old and gnarled,
Stooped with time,
Young and strong,
Together in a line.

Dwarves of all ages,
Many generations,
Sizes and colours,
From different nations.

United in the time of war,
Armour gleaming in the sun,
Blazing eyes, eager faces,
They would not leave till the battle was done.

The fight ensued,
With blood, guts and bark,
Yet it was all over
At the sounding of a lark.

Some fled, others bled,
One mourned the losing of a head,
Looking at the invalids,
I saw my friend, but he was dead.

With honour did brave Trevor die,
Fighting for what's right,
But now he rests, and sleeps,
In an everlasting night.

Forty years and forty more
Have passed since that day,
Only mouldering remains are left
Where brave Trevor lay.

I still hear his voice, his sorrowful song,
That haunting melody,
It comes to me on lonely nights,
Reminding me of he.

I regret that he had to die,
Whilst I stood and looked on,
But memories are all that's left,
Because Trevor is gone.

Lois Rawlins (13)
St Peter's School, Bournemouth

The Ghost Child

I mourn and mourn 'til day is done.
Upon the heath was when it had begun.
On a cool spring day, on summer's eve,
I was sitting upon a heath
Looking at the lake with fish below.

Boys with their fathers
Fishing on one side of the lake
And I, alone, on the other.
I stood up as a great gale blew
And I was tossed into the fishy lake below.

It was a long and painful death,
For I was bitten by an eel,
But that day, 'twas long ago.
Days later, fishermen found my dead,
Lifeless corpse cemented in sand -
Far from the lake.

So now, in my ghostly form,
Forgotten by my mother and father,
I sit on the heath,
Looking at the lake with fish below.
Boys with their fathers
Fishing on one side,
And I, alone, on the other.

I am the ghost child.
Alone.
Forever . . .

Charlotte Wragg (12)
St Peter's School, Bournemouth

The Runaway Boy

It was Monday morning
When in December fell
Then Nathan woke up in a fright
When he remembered the bell

His face as thick as clay
He wiped the soot off his coat
His hair was chestnut brown
His eyes clear as day

'Nathan you're late for work!'
Groaned his tired old mother
He jumped from stair to stair
When he gave a smirk to his brother

'Stay away from the gang,' quoted she
Road from road, street to street
Once again he was late
But he smiled, whistled to the sea

He worked hours on end
There stood the jet-black chimneys
Dirt and soot all around
Left Nathan round the bend

'Did you hear about the mayor's house?'
Quoted one of the gang members
They all peered around Nathan
He was as silent as a mouse

He thought about his mum
He could win or he could lose
He thought about all that booze
Could the horrible deed be done?

'OK' he said in thought
Hours later it passed
They smuggled down to the port
They went to the boat which they bought

They rowed in the pitch-black
The boat moving side to side
The wind blowing in their faces

Past Poets - Future Voices Visions Of Youth

Whilst Nathan was stretching his back

'Is that he?' quoted a soul
'Is that the runaway boy?'
'Well the promise has been broken'
'The boy's heart is not a hole'

They entered the damp marsh
Their feet were covered in wet mud
'Nathan there it is!' quoted Tom
They stumbled in the green grass

'Look at the food,' whispered Jake
The hot, juicy lamb covered in mint
Also hot, steamy vegetables
And also warm pasta bake

'Halt who goes there?' said the mayor
With his magma-hot head
His eyes as bright as the sun
Also his flaming, bright hair

'Son, send the dogs,' quoted he
The boys were all in shock
'Runaway!' cried the helpless boys
They tripped and stumbled in the woodlands

'We need to get to the boat!'
The muscular dogs were moving fast
They were tired and cold
The only protection was a coat

The dogs took a nasty bite
'Nathan!' screamed one member
He lay there with hardly a life
His blood reflected in the moonlight

All the boys ran and fled
There lay Nathan battered
He was weeping in pain
He looked almost half-dead

Here was an almost bright light
Nathan felt warm and dry
Despite his hand was scratched

He tried to move it with all his might

'Well you are a lucky boy,'
The voice was sweet as honey
'Well I did take pity'
'One boy has died called Roy'

'Mum?' said Nathan with a tear
Her face lit up his heart
When he saw her not angry
'O Nathan, it's me dear'

He saw his family with flowers
He told about the story
How they forced him a sin
It seemed it went for hours

The large church bell rang
People crying for the gang
The boys weeping for what they did
For the church choir sang

One boy survived and that was Nathan
Two days later, the rest were dead
The deed was completely done
The boys fell one by one.

Thomas Greenfield (13)
St Peter's School, Bournemouth

My Little Mouse

There is a little mouse
He lives inside my house
He's made his room in the wall
He will come out if you call

My friend came round for the day
With my mouse, we thought we'd play
We called and called but he never came
I was sad, it was such a shame

My mouse had gone on holiday
Packed his bags and gone away
Far away from home he went
Until his money was all spent

He returned last weekend
Not on his own but with a friend
I think he has taken a wife
I hope he has a lovely life

Now he never comes when I call
He doesn't play with me at all
As long as he's happy I don't mind
But when he pops his head round, he's still kind.

Sinead Tickner (12)
St Peter's School, Bournemouth

Lola

It was early one morning,
Though a cloud hung high and didn't hide,
Above this family's head,
A storm was brewing inside.

A little girl sat helpless,
Her mother storming about in a craze.
Her father, she did not know,
A tear rolled down her face, lost in a daze.

She had done nothing wrong,
Just her sad existence.
Sad, among her few belongings
To her mother, just an annoying persistence.

Nothing she did was right,
But she still tried her hardest
To impress her mother,
Who thought of her as worthless.

But one day, when she arrived home from school,
Her mother away, but would be home soon,
She rummaged through an unclosed drawer,
Left open, in her mother's room.

She stared at a box,
Tied carefully in golden ribbon.
Dare she open it?
For her mother's room was forbidden.

As the golden ribbon untied,
A dramatic past she was to see
A picture of her mother,
As happy as could be.

She was holding a child,
A handsome man by her side,
The child, a boy,
Had a huge smile, happy and wide.

Past Poets - Future Voices Visions Of Youth

Who is this? young Lola wondered,
Why is mother not happy with me.
Is it me she does not like,
Is it me who makes her unhappy?

Bang! The front door slammed,
Lola shoved the box back,
But the ribbon was untied.
The stairs went *creak, crack.*

Her mother entered and saw Lola hiding there,
She screamed with rage, though almost with fear.
'What have you done?' she shrieked at Lola.
Down Lola's face ran a tear.

But then the most extraordinary thing happened,
Lola's mother broke down and cried.
Clutching Lola in her arms,
Hunching over Lola, also trying to hide.

Her mother explained
Where she had been to Lola.
'The man in the photo was Darren
And our baby boy, Miller.'

'I lost them both in a car accident,
Then I found I was pregnant with you.
I never got over the devastation,
I was often out drinking till two.'

Then she picked up and left
And strolled out of the door,
Shouting up the stairs, 'Dinner at six
And all the washing to be done before.'

Lola got up and followed suit,
But she knew it was not over yet.
Better days were going to get better,
And dried her face that was all wet.

Lilith Riley (13)
St Peter's School, Bournemouth

The Secret Letter

Among the cobwebbed attic treasures
Memories of many past years
Books and pictures, notes well weathered
Some brought laughter, some brought tears.

She rummaged through the souvenirs
For hours and hours did go by
Childhood friends and high school proms
Her first real date had gone in a sigh.

Then she stumbled on a box
Of keepsakes from her mother, May
Little secret, well kept treasures
Opened now in light of day.

She read the letters from her father
Words of love that brought her tears
She walked back through her mother's youth
Recapturing the long lost years.

One more letter left unopened
At the bottom of the box
She sat and stared at it in wonder
Brushing back her golden locks.

Dare she read the secret letter
From her mother's secret youth?
This box of uncovered treasures
Thirst for knowledge of the truth.

She tore the envelope wide open
Pulled the letter from inside
And in the misty attic air
She read it slowly as she cried

It was a letter full of love
Not written in her father's hand
Addressed 'Dear Rosebud' at the top
A letter from another man.

It told of his undying love
And promised her that he would be
Beside her always in this life

And ever through eternity.

The letter was unsigned of course
And barely finished in its haste
The ink was stained with teardrops
Of a love that now had gone to waste.

She'd had a vision of her mother
Only seen in photographs
And always looking like an angel
Full of love and joyful laughs.

And now the vision had been shattered
Now the truth had been exposed
A letter to a 'Rosebud'
And her mother was the lovely rose.

She took the letter to her father
Her tears revealed the truth that she knew
Her mother had another love
This depressing thought made her blue.

Her father tearfully nodded
Trembling as he read the page
He said sometimes the written word
Reveals the truth from that age.

He held her tight and said these words
This secret I already knew
This letter's in your mother's hand
The 'Rosebud', darling, it was you.

Danielle Magnien (12)
St Peter's School, Bournemouth

The Day I Die

I take one final look below,
As I prepare myself for death.
The noose around my neck
In the bell tower above the heath.

My memories flicker back
To the hours that flew by
To the moment I found my lover,
Stolen from my heart so sly.

'Katie!'
His voice caught the wind,
I felt his presence near,
I felt his touch on my skin.

'Katie!'
I thought of how he betrayed me,
My heart hurt so bad
That I knew who could stop the pain. Destiny.

'Destiny! Destiny!' I cried out loud,
In hope that he would hear me
And stop the pain inside my heart.
Destiny.

The sun now rises in the sky,
Only one thing I lack,
My lover standing by my side,
This is my final act

My heart now races in my chest,
Still one thing I lack,
Courage that helps me concentrate
Whilst I commit my suicidal act.

I see his figure around me,
I think of all you did.
I imagine what life would be like
If I tried to forgive.

My heart races and is in my mouth,
My head aches and pounds.
My ears hear his voice

As I imagine life on ground.

Destiny is in my mind,
Destiny is in my heart,
Destiny is in my life
And I must play my part.

Together as one
I thought we were,
I used to think this true
But now I stand so still
Thinking back to how we were through.

There it is, around my neck
Like an ever tightening scarf.
I wonder if they will find me,
If they will weep or laugh.

This is the moment,
I have not wept.
My time has run out,
I take my final step. . .

Rhianna Metcalfe (13)
St Peter's School, Bournemouth

The Girl At The End Of My Bed

There she sits at the end of my bed,
The icy winter wind blowing through the curtains.
She just sits and stares, watching me all hunched up
Underneath my covers scared stiff.
She stands up.
A shiver runs through my spine.
I watch her come towards me.
My heart is pounding, pounding, pounding.
She reaches her arms out towards me, I cry for help,
My voice trembling with fear, but no one can hear me.
I suffer alone, I suffer alone and in silence.

Bethany Emerton (12)
St Peter's School, Bournemouth

The Creation

The black empty space stretched on,
No light lit up the sky,
No wind did blow in empty space,
No beast or bird did fly.

But a gentle voice did speak,
And his gentle voice did blow,
His spirit lived in empty space,
There were changes down below.

On the very first day,
His mind created light.
Dark was night and light was day,
The light which shone so bright.

Then on the second day,
The light lit up the sky,
Its colours always changing,
It stretched on so very high.

Then on the following day,
He separated water and land.
He named water sea, and land Earth,
Created by His mighty hand.

God commanded, 'Come up, plants.'
They began to climb up tall,
They produced grain and bore fruit.
Life brought to an end in the fall.

Then on the fourth day,
'Let there be lights in the night sky,
They will give light to the Earth.'
But they will die one day.

But then ever big lights,
They ruled over day and night.
With the day rose the sun,
With the moon came silver light.

His next command was made,
Let there be life in the seas,
And the skies be filled with life.
He blessed them and was pleased.

Evening passed and dawn came,
Let animals come forth from Earth,
Large, small and it was done.
No measure to what it's worth.

'We will make human beings,
Who rule over beast and bird.'
He made them in His image,
The voice of God they heard.

Now the blue sky stretched on,
The light lit up the skies,
Now wind did blow, no empty space,
Now bird and beast do fly.

Now man and bird and beast rejoice,
God's breath as light as a feather.
They sing together a joyful song,
To Him who lives forever.

Daniel Nascimento
St Peter's School, Bournemouth

I Am A Soldier

I am a soldier,
Now war is declared.
My mum I have told her,
So now she is scared.

I made a big decision,
Signing the petition.
I'm going to get a gun,
And rounds of ammunition.

The equipment is great,
The hygiene is not.
If I die, that is fate,
The plan could go to pot.

I'm now in my dugout,
The only place of rest.
I'm usually up and about,
Filling sandbags is the best.

We've set up the trenches,
With no-man's-land in between.
There are already stenches,
By gas that can't be seen.

I've made some good mates
All from the same town.
We set up the G8s,
And laid the sandbags down.

We have now started,
Bombarding Germans with shells.
Already people have parted,
No funerals, no bells.

Bodies are all around,
Their stench is everywhere.
Corpses in the ground,
Yet nobody gives a care.

Past Poets - Future Voices Visions Of Youth

I wish the shells would stop,
They're giving people shellshock.
Then we'd go over the top,
Time's running out, *tick-tock*.

The artillery's silent,
After a week of firing.
It's going to be violent,
It's going to be tiring.

I'm going over the parapet,
The Germans' guns are ready.
The barbed wire like a net,
The Germans' guns are ready.

I was lying down in mud,
With my pair of pliers.
People falling with a thud,
Trying to cut the barbed wires.

Then a hand grenade landed
In the mud beside my head.
I felt like I was branded,
Instead, I was dead.

Patrick McManus (12)
St Peter's School, Bournemouth

The Battle

The fight was nearing
And there was a silence as the men waited.
Soon there would be blood spilled,
They could hear the enemy army approaching, who they hated.

Men and children stared,
Archers got their bows ready,
Knights held their heads high,
Holding their swords steady.

The enemy could be seen from above the great city,
The archers aimed, holding their bows still,
A loud cry could be heard as the enemy horses charged,
The captain ordered the archers to fire at will.

There were millions of arrows raining down from the sky,
The men on the horses were battered,
The shower of arrows went on for an hour,
Now the enemy's ranks were tattered.

Now they charged at the enemy good and hard,
There were at least a thousand men charging,
The sound was loud and ferocious,
The men went in swinging.

The battle looked to be going well,
The second line of men were sent into the battle,
They fought hard, giving the enemy a lot of hassle,
They shredded them to pieces like they were cattle.

This was not the end of the battle,
The enemy had a route to put more troops into battle,
The second line of troops were not in a big enough number to fight,
There was no choice but to use the city guards, hearing their swords rattle.

They marched to the valley where the enemy's troops were coming,
The guards were only 200 in number.
The enemy had 2,000 left,
The guards were ready to fight fiercely and put enemies into eternal slumber.

The guards fought like warrior gods, killing wave after wave of enemy,
They were fighting hard, slashing
Into their armour and flesh.
Still the enemy went on crashing and smashing.

The battle had nearly ended, only five guards remained against 20 enemies.
The guards died bravely fighting,
Now no guards remained, but only ten of the enemy were left.
The ten fled, scared of the will of the guards, thinking of them as frightening.

Now the battle had been won,
Many were lost and gone.
The will of these guards is praised
And in times of need we pray to them for their spirit of battle that once shone.

Andrew Sackett (13)
St Peter's School, Bournemouth

Moo Cow

I woke up late one morning,
And heard my mother laugh,
I ran downstairs to see her,
Before my morning bath.

I called out, 'Mum, where are you?'
She called back, 'Down below.'
I looked around to see her
And saw a fiendish glow.

Upon the kitchen counter
Sat my mother, in a chair,
The size of this just shocked me,
It was as if she wasn't there.

She sat there quite collected,
Composed and tranquil too,
The movements quite bemused me,
Then she let out a great moo.

At first I was quite astonished,
Abashed, bewildered, dazed,
That my mother, whom I knew,
Would come out as if quite crazed.

How could my mother keep this
From those she truly loved?
That she was once a moo cow,
The ones that once were gloved.

These cows were ones that made it,
That ran afar from love,
Along the grassy midlands,
Trapped inside a glove.

The moo cows of the midlands
Inside were churned like clover,
That's why people loved them,
From Spain to the fields of Dover.

Past Poets - Future Voices Visions Of Youth

My mum began to moo
So loud I almost cried,
Her moo was oh so piercing,
I almost nearly died.

So I grabbed my mum so tightly,
And she flew across the room,
She landed in the toilet
And I hit her with a broom.

I flushed the loo so harshly,
The moo was hurting me,
I couldn't stand how she made me feel,
The moo forced me to flee.

I ran straight to my bedroom
And crawled into my bed,
I went straight back to sleep tight,
To rest my flummoxed head.

Ellen Higgins (13)
St Peter's School, Bournemouth

Fate

Lurking beneath the ground,
Its existence unnoticed,
A large, hideous beast
Is there, not even noticed.

Now severely threatened,
The Minotaur lives on.
People are going to find him,
They will ensure he is gone.

Not worried about his fate,
The Minotaur gets ready.
Prepared for blood and battle,
He thinks people are greedy.

People are tracking him down,
With big grins upon their face.
Are they going to find him?
They are increasing the pace.

They are getting very close,
Now on the city's border,
The spooky trees are looming,
Trying to maintain order.

They approach a steep cliff,
Inside, the Minotaur waits.
Trying to find a way in,
They question their own fate.

The clouds begin to open up,
Rain falls at a high rate.
The people think for a way in,
The Minotaur shows his fate.

The people launch their arrows,
Trying to get a good shot.
The Minotaur kills someone,
Avoiding most of the shots.

Finally, he is struck,
A nasty one, in his heart,
He is bleeding away,
He tries to do something smart.

A human should not kill him,
He takes his final chance.
Off the cliff he does go,
The humans watch, in a trance.

The Minotaur, now a myth,
The last of its kind gone,
Its body is no more,
Even though its soul lives on.

Gianpiero Placidi (13)
St Peter's School, Bournemouth

This Dark Place

Walking through the rain back home from school,
Winter's coldness so picking up my pace,
Stepping through the puddles,
Because there is no race.

iPod turning up so full,
Drowning out the sound,
Watching groups of people huddle,
Looking at nothing; but the ground.

Heading through the park, everything is still,
Except the one group talking loud,
They're dressed in black - all in black,
Getting scared, my heart begins to pound.

Staring at me, just staring,
Seeing through the corner of my eye,
One walking over to no one else but me,
I keep walking as if it's all a lie.

Seeing that figure standing in front of me,
I stop still; he looks me in the eye,
I was feeling more than fear,
Just terror and I will not cry.

He walks away, I walk ahead,
Showing no fear, my head held high,
But still aware of his presence,
Trying to breathe; in one big sigh.

iPod still booming, hood still up,
Beginning to run - being drowned in rain,
Home is near; he is out of sight,
I feel nothing but pain . . .

Shock hits my back,
I gasp for breath, I scream for help,
But I am gone
And he is here.

I am now a soul lifted from my body,
The grin on his face,
The laughter of his gang,

I am dead and he has no grace.

I watch from my soul him running away,
My blood surrounds my body,
I cry and cry, but no tears leave me,
For I am now this; and always will be . . .

Yasmin Reid (13)
St Peter's School, Bournemouth

Jill's New House

Jill did not know what was coming
She went in her new house running
Her house was a great big mansion
This was the house for Jill Fashion

Jill got a dog from her mum
It would put its paw up if you said thumb
She had always wanted this poodle
And had always dreamed of calling it Noodle

Little did she know the house was haunted
If she found out, she would be daunted
There were corpses and bones on the roof
This house was truly not ghost-proof

There were goblins at the windows
And zombies with crossbows
There were monsters by the door
And warriors, who were ready for war

Jill went to bed after a great day
She thought about the house, where she lay
Something was licking her hand, it seemed to tickle
It was probably Noodle being a pickle

When Jill woke up she saw that something had died
Noodle was dead, oh how Jill cried
She went to the bathroom to go to the loo
Written in blood on the wall it said, 'Humans can lick too'.

James Flynn (13)
St Peter's School, Bournemouth

The Real Princess

It was a Saturday morning
A young, handsome man sitting beneath a tree
Watched a caterpillar crawl along the branch
Talking to his favourite bumblebee.

Thought to himself, the land would be happier if there was a real princess
He told his bumblebee, Jeffrey, about this
They travelled till they would find a princess
But none of them would seem right for him to kiss.

One day the worst ice storm hit the land
It came at such a strange time of year
The storm grew worse than ever before
So he went down to drink a cup of beer.

After a few minutes
Someone was knocking on the entrance of the house
He put on his robes and dashed to the door
A real princess, standing in the cold, said
'I'm lost in the storm and my throat is sore.'

The queen said, 'You must let her in'
She was very unkind and in a mood
Queen never told anyone about the magic peas
She never told the king because he was rude.

She called for the servants to bring 20 mattresses
The mattress was placed on top of the magic peas
The princess found it hard to sleep
She tried to have a dream about bees.

Next morning she asked the princess about her sleep
The princess burst into tears
No matter where she put her head
She thought it was like sleeping on some deer!

She realised the queen had done this
The queen said sorry and wouldn't do this again to her
The queen said she was beautiful and honest
So she offered her some myrrh.

They were making each other laugh by telling jokes
The princess was happy because the queen was in laughter
The prince entered and they both fell in love
And they all lived happily ever after.

Sharon Thompson (13)
St Peter's School, Bournemouth

I Love You

I love you with all my heart,
And I know we shall never part.
You are mine and I am yours,
And we together can open many doors.

I love you because you care for me,
And in this time you will see
That I care for you too,
Even when you don't, I do.

I love you because I can,
Because you came and never ran.
So if you really love me too,
I will know that you are true.

I love you with all my heart,
And I know we shall never part.
You are mine and I am yours
And together we can open many doors.

Francesca Whitaker (12)
St Peter's School, Bournemouth

A Pain Of Love

The words he spoke so softly
Are always in my mind,
When I think back to that night
It sends a shiver down my spine.

The darkness, mist in the air,
The rustling through the trees,
The dark and gloomy atmosphere,
And the cool of the breeze.

The way we walked,
Hand in hand,
Brings back the memories
Of myself and he on this land.

But our peace came to an end
When the forest turned against
The love that we shared,
His muscles tensed.

They came towards us
With their spikes, horns and teeth,
They crowded us and snarled,
Whilst we stared across the heath.

I know I used to love him,
I know I still do now,
I remember the moment when I saw
The goblins take a bow.

His body lying on the ground.
Only pieces left of him.
His love was torn right from my heart.
I will remember him.

Samantha Keating (13)
St Peter's School, Bournemouth

Hamster

This tiny little creature
Is not a very big feature
She goes to sleep in the day
And awakes at night to play.

She charges around all night
Any predator she will bite
When she needs something to eat
She will not go to sleep.

She waits to be taken out
If nobody comes she will shout
Climbing into her cosy house
She is like a mouse.

There she sits, on her own
If she is lonely she will moan
Waiting for the night to pass
The morning is coming fast

The big bright sun begins to rise
There she says her goodbyes
The humans begin to get up
And take a shower to warm up.

She realises her time is here
She sets herself into gear
To get back into her bed
And she goes to sleep in her shed.

This tiny little creature
Is not a very big feature
She goes to sleep in the day
And awakes at night to play.

Michael Laking (13)
St Peter's School, Bournemouth

A Child's Tears

She wakes up alone
As cold as ice
To find nobody's home
She lives without the comforting advice.

She has little food
With no way of getting it
Everyone's so rude
But she never wants to admit it.

Her parents are never home
She lives all alone
Tired and cold
Left there to die
To live alone.

Her school day is no better
She sits alone
Writing a letter
She is as thin as bone.

As the snow starts to lay
And it begins to rain
Her ambitions turn to ice
And in floods the pain.

She's lonely inside
And can't hide it on the outside
Her eyes are wide open
With the past gleaming beside.

Her mind is trembling
With her future overwhelming
The thoughts in her mind were crescending
With her heart breaking
But she never wants to admit it.

Her parents are never home
She lives all alone
Tired and cold
Left there to die
To live alone.

She's all alone
As darkness surrounds her
She's all alone
As fear surrounds her.

Her time has come to an end
For her spirit to be free with the wind
Her parents betrayed her
And now she'll never be alone.

Abi Harmsworth (14)
Skinners' Kent Academy, Tunbridge Wells

Broken

How could you do this to me?
You said we were forever,
But you lied.
You took my hand and said goodbye
Now I weep to myself in my room.

You couldn't give a damn if you broke my heart
Because you've got her now.
I try to forget you
But everything I do reminds me of you.
I try to run
But it makes no difference
Because you're still there, in my head.

When someone breaks your heart
I'm going to laugh.

I will never forget you
I try to
But I know I never will.

You broke my heart
Now I'm going to break you.

Holly Martin (13)
Skinners' Kent Academy, Tunbridge Wells

A Mole In A Hole

When it is wet
I am happy
But when it is dry
I am not
I like the day and I like the dark
It is the world I live in
I am all alone
But when I see the stars in the dark blue sky
I know that I am being smiled upon
But when I feel down
I know that I will come up
And be with someone who is my god
Their specks shine on me
But I go down
I go back to digging in the wet ground
Some people say I am vermin
When I come up in their garden
But I am doing what I need to
Maybe I am like a rat
But a rat cannot make a hole
Like I do
That is why I am known as . . .
The 'digger' of the animal world
If you cannot tell what I am
Look down through the hole in your back garden
And see if you can tell . . .
That a mole has left you a pile of mud.

Daniel Barrett (13)
Skinners' Kent Academy, Tunbridge Wells

The Teddy Bear

I am a quiet little teddy bear
Sitting on my own
Waiting for my friends and family
To come home.

I sit on my own
Curled up in the corner
When no one else
Is home.

I wish someone would come
To pick me up
And keep me safe.

Finally they are home
Now I am not alone
She runs straight for me
Picking me up and keeping me warm.

I look in her indigo eyes
As they glisten in the golden light.

She puts me under her soft, feather blanket
And waves at me as she goes downstairs.

That little girl comes back up the stairs
To check on me
She crawls into bed with me by her side
She kisses me on the cheek
As we fall asleep.

Charlotte Taylor (11)
Skinners' Kent Academy, Tunbridge Wells

Rain

There is rain on the green grass
And rain on the tree
And on the house top
But not on me!

James Jenner (13)
Skinners' Kent Academy, Tunbridge Wells

Angel Made Of Stone

There's a little girl on the end of Chimney Street,
She has but two swollen feet,
Rags or drags whichever suits you,
You hear that happy bird tweet but,
No one hears that little girl weep.

There's a little girl on the end of Chimney Street,
Her mummy died when she was just five,
That's when her step-daddy took hold,
He told that helpless little girl to go.
No one hears that little girl cry.

There's a little girl on the end of Chimney Street,
Nowhere to go, no one to help.
She sat on the end of Chimney Street,
No one hears that little girl cry, but why?

There's a little girl on the end of Chimney Street,
Curled up trying to keep warm,
Angel of stone she is,
Would you like to end up like this?
Just try to hear that little girl cry.

There's a little girl on the end of Chimney Street,
She now rests at God's feet,
The angels named her sweetly,
Angel of stone,
For once in that little girl's life someone answered her prayers!

Bethan Pierce (14)
Skinners' Kent Academy, Tunbridge Wells

Soldiers

Soldiers, soldiers keep us safe,
Make us proud and keep the faith,
Do a good job and fight for what's right,
Do what you're best at; fight.

Brogan Malyon (14)
Skinners' Kent Academy, Tunbridge Wells

My Life

My dad yelling
Mum head banging
Jade crying
Stefan lying
Courtney grassing
This is my life

My door knocking
My mate waiting
I'm asking
My dad confusing
This is my life

I'm out playing
My phone ringing
It's my dad calling
I am talking
While we are walking
This is my life

We are walking
We are stopping
We are in the woods climbing
I'm in a tree looking
I'm falling
My ribs and fingers are hurting
This is my brilliant and dreadful life.

Jordan Wilson (12)
Skinners' Kent Academy, Tunbridge Wells

Remembrance Day

This is for the soldiers
The ones who fight in war,
All the loved ones we have lost,
Due to actions in the war.

The only way we remember
Is to wear one poppy
Or maybe two.

This is for the soldiers
The ones who fight in war,
All the loved ones we have lost,
Due to actions in the war.

You must remember
The 11th November
To thank all of them
Who fought in war.

This is for the soldiers
The ones who fight in war,
All the loved ones we have lost,
Due to actions in the war.

God bless them
And thank you,
You saved us
With your bravery.

Geordie Starling (13)
Skinners' Kent Academy, Tunbridge Wells

Love

Never say hi
If you really mean bye
Never say 'I love you'
If you don't really mean it
Never hold my hand
If you are only going to crush my heart
Never talk about feelings
If they are not really there
Never gaze into my eyes
Without grinning that smile
If you are only going to lie
Never say forever.
If you really mean never
Never say you will try
I will always know when you lie
Never say forever
Because forever makes me cry
You broke my heart once
That wasn't enough
You broke my heart twice
That is enough
Now as I lie here in pain and sorrow
You start to feel the same way I do
All this time I felt alone
Now we are together heart in stone.

Chantelle Streeter (12)
Skinners' Kent Academy, Tunbridge Wells

Sweet Dreams

In my dream, lollipops were trees,
That had starburst leaves,
Kit-Kat bar pavements
And SKA blazers that I wore to school.

When it rained, Jelly Tots fell from the sky,
In the winter, marshmallows were snow,
Candy floated through the sky.

Chocolate brownies were the rocky mountains,
Pink wafer fish swam by in the chocolate lake,
Jelly worms were slithering by in all different shapes and sizes.

The moon was a bright, white gobstopper,
Skittles were my dress,
Red liquorice sticks for pencils,
All the school walls tasted of strawberry!

I went through a forest,
Shooting magic stars lit the night sky,
And Galaxy bears were just passing by.

I entered a mysterious cave,
When I heard my brother call me,
I woke up and my brother was standing next to me, trying to wake me up.
I didn't want to wake up!

Charlie Brooker (13)
Skinners' Kent Academy, Tunbridge Wells

Time

Tick-tock, I'm a clock
I tell the time and never whine
Tick-tock, it's 9 o'clock
The lamplighter shouts, 'All is fine.'

People rush back from work to rest
Time flies, ready for tomorrow's surprise.

Rhys Watts (11)
Skinners' Kent Academy, Tunbridge Wells

Fears And Terrors

Trapped, captured, what have I done?
Behind bars, my fate has been won!

Staring, stalking,
Fed through a cage,
My legs are restless,
I wish to roam again.

I turn, I run,
But I am put back in place,
Creatures with lights come visit my cage!

I hate to admit it -
My fears have been found,
Roars and shouts are the only way out.

Jangling keys,
Doors slamming all night,
How do I take this?
I have no might.

Prison is a terrible place!

Ellie Brooker (13)
Skinners' Kent Academy, Tunbridge Wells

Beauty

Roses are red
Apples are green
You're the prettiest lady I've ever seen.

Give me your number
Give me a shout
Then you will find out what my life's about.

Roses are red
Apples are green
I love you more than my 40 inch plasma screen.

Joshua Hamilton (12)
Skinners' Kent Academy, Tunbridge Wells

Night-Time Cat

The cool night air brushes against my fur,
The sound of silence whistles in the wind.

I hear footsteps, the sound fills the dark streets,
Isolated shadows haunt the pavements.

A flickering street lamp dims to darkness,
An old lady walks by and strokes my head.

Humming to herself, she sits beside me,
Holding out her small, prune-like hand, she speaks.

She whispers in my ear, her whole life story,
Silent tears trickle down her filthy face.

Purring softly, I nuzzle against her,
Placing her hands in her pockets, she stands.

'Night, Puss,' she says, then slowly vanishes,
'Night,' I purr softly, but no one hears me.

So I sit, waiting for the next person's story,
But I fear they will never hear mine.

Francesca Drewett (12)
Skinners' Kent Academy, Tunbridge Wells

The Mushroom Cloud

A big, black bubble in the sky
A cloud that is ever so high
What's that? What's that? People sigh
But the big, black bubble in the sky
Won't go away, not tomorrow, not today.

Ash on the floor, on people's clothes and everywhere,
Millions of people die and still people sigh
That big, black bubble in the sky
Just won't fly.

Kelsey-Marie Stanford (12)
Skinners' Kent Academy, Tunbridge Wells

I Am A Bird!

I am a bird,
Flying far, far away,
Fluttering my wings as I sway.

Now I am
Trapped in a cage,
What can I do as I age?

What else can I do?
I have water and food,
Warmth and shelter,
But I'm never in the mood.

It's either me or you,
How would you like it if you were
My cell mate too?

I know what I can do,
I can fly away for an hour or two!
I wish my reality was just a dream,
But all I can do is scream!

Jasmine Gower (12)
Skinners' Kent Academy, Tunbridge Wells

My Colourful Kite

Red, black, blue and green,
These are the colours I have seen,
Orange, purple, silver, white,
These are the colours of my kite.

Flying up really high,
Letting the wind drift it - bye.
Up, up, there it goes,
Where it falls, nobody knows.

Summer Woodcraft (11)
Skinners' Kent Academy, Tunbridge Wells

A Life Without Happiness

My past, present and future,
Surrounded by misery and tears.
Through the journey
I went
Down a small, narrow path
All alone.

A lonely soul
Searching for happiness.
I still search to this day.
When I think
Have I made a wrong choice?
Was it God's fault?
I know no one is to blame
Just me, me alone.
I'm getting old now
Waiting to die,
Will I find happiness?
It must be a lie.

Lliam Grant (12)
Skinners' Kent Academy, Tunbridge Wells

The Race Driver

Sitting on the first grid slot
Building up the revs a lot
The lights go out and we're away
I really hope I win today
We all go into the first turn
Someone crashes, I hope he'll learn.

I come in for my one pit stop
I change, my tyres go pop!
A blue flag is waved to someone at the back
To move out the way of me on the track
The final lap has been completed
All the other drivers have been defeated.

Jacob Court (11)
Skinners' Kent Academy, Tunbridge Wells

Me And My Pets

My pets mean the world to me,
I have guinea pigs, a total of 4,
Cuddles is my favourite,
He lies on his back on the floor!

I have a cat, cute as can be,
Her name is Suga and she loves Mummy and me.
She loves playing in the grass, chasing all the flies,
Especially when she's under the sunny, blue skies.

My dog is called Rascal,
He is my friend,
We go for long walks,
But he drives me round the bend!

My hamster is called Lulu,
She is as mad as can be.
She jumps from floor to floor,
She chews loudly on the bars
And tries so hard to get out the door.

Paige Clark (12)
Skinners' Kent Academy, Tunbridge Wells

Night And Day

The owl sits in the night,
Sees all without any light.
He senses movement in the grass,
He zooms down quick and very fast.

As the sun begins to rise,
People start movement with the fires.
I can see lots of flies,
Rising up higher and higher.

Jack Attwater (12)
Skinners' Kent Academy, Tunbridge Wells

Remembrance

Eleventh of the eleventh,
Is a day to remember,
For the bravery and intrepidity
In the month of November.

For all the poppies we wear,
And the feelings we share,
Eleventh of the eleventh is an
Important day to
Remember.

And still,
Will,
Never be forgotten.

I may shed a tear,
You may even cry,
But we hold our heads up together
And salute them
Goodbye.

Yasmeen Soudani (14)
Skinners' Kent Academy, Tunbridge Wells

A Dog's Life

I lie in the sunshine,
Happier than I'll ever be,
Trying to catch the bees as they go by.
I watch my owner cutting the grass,
I move so I'm not in the way.

He throws the ball for me,
I run and catch my target.
I'm tired again, I lie down and relax.

Lucy Bickmore (12)
Skinners' Kent Academy, Tunbridge Wells

Life!

Life is like a flower, it is unknown.
It begins from a seed and it grows,
Tall and strong or small and weak,
No one knows!

Life is tough,
But it does have its ups and downs,
Never give up,
As success is all around.

Life is great with friends and family,
They are always there
And love . . .
It is also there,
Here to stay
With passion and care.

Life is you and me . . .
Put together like a family.

Casey Ansell (12)
Skinners' Kent Academy, Tunbridge Wells

The Rhino

My skin is grey,
As rough as leather,
I have a horn
On the end of my nose,
I use it to charge down my foes.

You may find me in Africa or perhaps Asia.
I defend my child
Until he knows our ways,
But I have one sorrow
Caused by you,
That me, my child and my child's child
Will soon find our heads
On a poacher's wall.

Harry Clark (12)
Skinners' Kent Academy, Tunbridge Wells

The Wind

The wind blows roughly against my face,
Whilst the leaves scatter with a quiet grace,
I sit there and watch the swings blow,
Then I sit there and let my mind just flow.

There are so many things the wind can do,
I can get confused and not have a clue.
Then if you relax you will start to see
That the wind can do many things for me.

The sound of the wind reminds me of many things,
The birds flying high with graceful wings,
With fluffy, white clouds floating high above
And saints and angels of the ones I love.

The wind is not seen, but you know it's there,
Travelling memories and love in the air,
It can be wild and strong, warm or cold,
And each breeze carries a tale to be told.

Ria Sellings (12)
Skinners' Kent Academy, Tunbridge Wells

Runaway Dad

You say you love me,
So why do you leave?
You run as fast as a cheetah,
Though not from me.
The thing you run from is just responsibility!

There is one thing I do not understand,
You said you wanted me,
So why, like a turtle, bury me in the sand?

How I wish I could give you a hug,
Or a steaming hot coffee in a mug.
But you are not here, that makes me sad.
You ran away, Dad, that makes me mad!

Katie Gough (12)
Skinners' Kent Academy, Tunbridge Wells

Mobile Phone

I'm still,
I'm hard,
I'm slidey.

I'm a brick,
I'm a touch,
I'm a flip.

I'm anything you want me to be.

I can have games,
Music,
Calculator,
Internet.

Touch me,
Feel me.

I'm a phone,
A hard phone.

Sasha Fry (12)
Skinners' Kent Academy, Tunbridge Wells

Cats

Three little kittens,
All in a row,
Three little kittens,
Saying hello.

William, Sammy and Claudia,
Playing all together,
Playing with the dog,
My little Trevor.

Three little kittens,
All grown up,
Three little kittens,
Eating their chow chup.

Georgia Rayner (13)
Skinners' Kent Academy, Tunbridge Wells

Broken Hearted

You hurt me,
I cried.
You said, hey,
Which broke my heart.
You picked it up
Then tried to make it whole,
But broke it all over again
Just like yesterday.
You said we could be forever,
But you lied.
I was the fool
As I believed you.
All my friends said it wouldn't work,
I wish I'd listened,
But now I'm sitting here bleeding.
The wounds you gave me won't ever heal
Because of what I feel about you.

Meghan Edwards (12)
Skinners' Kent Academy, Tunbridge Wells

Holidays

H ome we are, cold and bored
O n our way to our hot destination
L anded finally at the airport
I ce cream melting in my hand
D ays going by like a whirlwind
A dip in the pool to cool you down
Y ellow, scorching hot sun in my eyes
S ad we are back on the plane going home.

Ellie Maynard (12)
Skinners' Kent Academy, Tunbridge Wells

I Hunt

I hunt for my food
Which would last me all week,
It does not matter whether
It is a deer or zebra,
Any other animal that
Catches my eye will do.

So, I sit . . . beneath the trees
Surrounded by humming bees,
Waiting for my prey . . .
Ready to kill.

I hear the thundering sounds
Of trees going down,
So I start to wonder,
How will my future be
Amongst this storming danger
Coming to steal my life?

Shifaul Ahmed (14)
Skinners' Kent Academy, Tunbridge Wells

Island Sunset

S hining blue sea
U mbrella sticks in people's drinks
N o noise, but the sound of the waves splashing
S ailors coming back on boats
E vening time is coming
T ime's running out.

Holly Wright (14)
Skinners' Kent Academy, Tunbridge Wells

Down Under

Those days when I am warm with my coat,
Free from the world,
And curled up in a ball.

Those days, when I jump on the bed,
With its crisp, white sheets,
Clean from the washing,
Fast asleep,
While someone is stroking my fur,
Then waking up to the sun shining on my coat.

Those days when I gradually move closer and closer
To the radiator,
Waiting for the biscuits to shake
And the time for me to make that sound . . .
Miaow!

Holly Freeman (13)
Skinners' Kent Academy, Tunbridge Wells

Friends

I love them,
They love me,
We're like a family.
We stick by each other,
Just like a child and their mother.
Best friends forever.

Not all friends are true ones,
Some will betray you.
But you know when they are true
Because they'll stand by you till the end.

My friends are great,
Especially my best mate.
They will help you get ready for a date,
Or make up lies when you're running late.

Martina Cooper (12)
Skinners' Kent Academy, Tunbridge Wells

The Man In The Garage

He sits there watching the world go by,
He sits all alone as if he's waiting to die!
He is isolated like a trapped animal,
Making no complaint of his captivity,
His only desire is 27 and 53.
With Arthur filling his body with pain,
He doubts he'll ever walk again.
The man just sits there, in the sty,
He sits all alone as if he's waiting to die.
He feels lonely and empty inside,
An old, battered shed is a good place to hide.
Michael and Mina are determined to save him,
He hasn't eaten in ages, and so is looking scarily slim.
But what's that bulge under his shoulder blades?
Will they find out before Arthur invades?
Who knows how long it will be until the shed collapses?
When it does, the mysterious man will be no more than ashes.
What is this creature, a man, monster, or bird?
Or perhaps just a lonely person longing to be heard?
Days, weeks and months go by,
But still he sits there as if he's just waiting to die.
The cobwebs and owl pellets don't seem to worry him,
But then neither does his foul breath and plaster-like skin.
Antibiotics, brown ale and scuttling spiders are odd cravings,
He is loved more than he knows, but still is in desperate need of saving.
Did he used to be an owl, and is it a human he became?
The only thing we know about him is that Skellig is his name . . .

Kayla Ellis (12)
The Knights Templar School, Baldock

Alice

What was that?
Oh I must've been imagining it,
For a minute there I thought it was -
There it is again.
A little white rabbit in a blue waistcoat.
It can't be,
Can it?
Surely not!
But where is he going?
And why is he holding a golden stop watch?
Perhaps I should follow him
Down the gloomy path,
To a proud, tall tree.
Down the hole.
I'm falling,
Falling.
Falling further and further down,
Into a bottomless pit.
It's as though the ground has swallowed me up,
There's no light.
Until . . .
Thud.
There's a pain in my head,
And I'm feeling slightly dizzy,
But I manage to stumble up.
I look around,
But all I see is doors,
And a small table.
I walk over to the table and I see
A rusty old key,
Cake and a drink that says:
'Drink me';
One sip can't harm me.
It's disgusting but suddenly,
I'm shooting up and up,
Until I hit my head.
I panic and reach out for the cake.

140

Past Poets - Future Voices Visions Of Youth

One bite and I start tumbling down,
I grab the key on my way.
Now, I'm small, tiny.
As small as a bug lost in a big world.
I look around and see a small door.
I walk towards it, shaking.
I look at the key in my hands.
It's the right size,
So perhaps I should see what happens.
And through I go,
Into a magical world.
There he is again,
The little rabbit.
Through the tall grass I go,
Bumping into vicious bugs on my way.
This must be a dream.
There's no way this is real.
I'm the size of a pea!
Running through this wild world
Has got me thinking.
What if life really was like this?
A completely opposite world.
Massive, threatening bugs,
Small girls running through grass,
Chasing after white rabbits in blue waistcoats.
This must be a dream!
It's so unrealistic.
The sad sky hanging over this miserable world,
The gloomy grass protecting the surface.
Where is this place?
It's so weird and wonderful,
It must be Wonderland.

Bethany Welch (14)
The Knights Templar School, Baldock

Red

In a home in Battersea,
Deep in London town,
A spooky canine mystery,
Trouble going down!

Someone let the dogs out,
Someone set them free,
But who was the culprit?
Whoever could it be?

Red was his name,
Freeing was his game.
Freeing his mates
Was the main aim.

He wanted a party
All night and day,
Nibble lots of food,
But he needed a way.

He poked his nose
Through the wire
To the button on the other side.
Oh how he loved to aspire.

Lucky, his mate,
Was the first to be released;
This was what he needed,
His agitation ceased.

The rest were released,
And they were going mad.
For the first time in their lives,
They were going to be bad.

Red, he's such a clever lad,
How did he break the lock?
The only thing he had broken before
Was a grandfather clock.

Nine of them were there that night,
All of them running free,
On their faces you could see

Wonderful, joyous glee.

So they took some action,
They set up CCTV.
They saw Red that night
Setting everyone free.

Red was caught red-handed,
His cage was made secure,
Oh no poor Red
Would never again be pure.

Red loves his new family
And the garden gnome.
What is even better,
Lucky has a home.

Adam Lunnon (13)
The Knights Templar School, Baldock

Snake

The snake is a deadly hunter
Its beady eyes
And long black tongue
Threatening to any creature with eyes
As its prey scuttles along
The snake becomes alert
It hides in the background
And waits
Hearing turns to vibration
Smell stronger than ever
Sight like a giant metal detector
The air turns to chocolate cake
Irresistible
The snake bursts into action
Sinking its fangs into
The feast
Like a vampire clone
That went terribly wrong.

Lauren Marshall (12)
The Knights Templar School, Baldock

Seasons

All four seasons bright in glory
Spring
Summer
Autumn
Winter
All bring joy and happiness to the world in so many different ways.

Spring brings warmth and flowers and lambs
The light begins to glisten off the water
Trees sway and people chatter, sitting on a picnic rug in the sun
Sheep and calves and baby ducklings gently hum in the distance
Flowers start to open up and stare at the sparkling frost
The air smells as sweet as iced buns
Spring is the birth of the sun.

Summer brings happiness and heat and joy
The sun beams down onto happy children playing
Splashing in the pool and having barbecues
Fun on the beach and sunbathing on the sand
You shiver and smile with joy and excitement
Children are animals with their toys
Summer is the birth of joy.

Autumn brings colours and rain and leaves
People walk while kicking the leaves as if they are footballs
Plodding along through the glorious mud
Red, yellow, green and orange
The trees are a rainbow of beauty
People say, 'It's never been duller'
Autumn is the birth of colour.

Winter brings snow and frost and happiness
Spending evenings under a blanket around the fire
Toasting marshmallows in the heat
Sipping soup and looking at the snow outside
Children play in the frost and snow
'Who can make the biggest snowman?'
'Me, me, me!'
We moan when it is cold
Winter is the birth of festivals.

All four seasons bright in glory
Spring
Summer
Autumn
Winter
All bring joy and happiness to the world in so many different ways!

Becky Ludbrook (12)
The Knights Templar School, Baldock

An Autumn Feeling

Autumn is a flame about to go out,
However it won't go down without a shout,
The leaves create a magnificent display,
Showing off a range of colours, a bright array.

The leaves rustle underneath my feet,
Like a never-ending brown paper sheet,
The nights are longer and days much shorter,
The sun we get has dropped by a quarter.

Put on your scarves and hats, we're told,
The teachers don't want us catching colds!
We quickly run from room to room,
As summer sunshine is replaced with gloom.

The birds fly around like elastic bands,
Gathering the food I threw from my hands,
We try to help them with regular feeds,
As they find it hard to gather their own seeds.

We start to notice the first frosts,
When we turn on the heating and realise the costs.
The wind blows through you like an icy dagger,
At times it is strong enough to make you stagger.

As October turns into November,
There is a night we should all remember.
Someone knocks on the door and makes you scream,
Get your pumpkins ready, it's Halloween!

Tom Picking (14)
The Knights Templar School, Baldock

Skellig Poem

There once was a beast who sat in a garage,
He was not small, yet not that large,
He sat there all day and he sat there all night,
But nothing seemed to ever give him a fright.

Some people say he's a big scary beast,
But he has never even hurt anyone, that is an at least,
We don't know what he is doing here,
And we have no clue why,
All I've heard of this mysterious creature
Is that he can fly.

There once was a beast who sat behind the sacks,
He never goes anywhere, although he has wings on his back,
He has a craving for Chinese food,
Twenty-seven and fifty-three,
He also drinks brown ale and gets it absolutely free,
Some people call him a thief,
And some call him a beast,
But what he really is
Is a creature of peace.

There once was a beast who had arthritis,
Some people said:
'He'll attack us and bite us',
He has to take cod liver oil and aspirin,
Whilst sitting quietly,
With no friends or any kin,
Personally I feel sorry for him,
After all he eats food out of the bin,
He is a suspicious little character,
All quiet and shy, it seems he does not care
Whether he'll live or die,
He is a complete opposite,
A monster that is shy,
He is a big scary creature
To you and dare I say I,

But inside he's just like
A miniscule curious little fly,
That is the end of my poem for now,
So I guess I will be saying ta-ra, cheerio, goodbye.

James Hazzard (12)
The Knights Templar School, Baldock

War

As I laid there in the dirt, everything was blurred,
Actions became slow and voices slurred,
As I laid there watching my team fight for their lives,
My heart breaks as my best friend dies.

Tahja Grimes (14)
The Knights Templar School, Baldock

Untitled

Skellig is as pale as a vampire, all dark and dim.
As he slowly rots away in a deep, dark shed
With bluebottles everywhere.
As Skellig was eating 27 and 53
Mina and Michael are doing all the work.

Callum Dungey (12)
The Knights Templar School, Baldock

Skellig Poem

A garage rotting away,
Down on Falconer Road,
A man's home is there,
Tucked away, away from the gloomy stares.

A man lies,
Lies in the garage,
He calls it home,
But it may not be soon.

His pale, white face,
His soft, gentle wings,
His old, creased clothes,
And his sulky, sad face.

His 27 and 53,
His aspirin and ale,
He drinks and eats,
But never moves,
From his desired place.

He doesn't move,
He refuses help,
All he wants to do is die,
Die quietly on his own.

He has arthritis,
And is feeling very poorly,
He is a very sick man,
Who does nothing about it.

As quiet as a mouse,
As dull as dirty water,
As gentle as a bunny rabbit,
As calm and cool as a cucumber.

He was moved away,
To a nearby house,
He is there on his own,
Just him, Skellig.

Matthew Dyne (12)
The Knights Templar School, Baldock

The Fly

The little fly on my window
Has been there since I came
Its empty little body
Lies there all the same

When I used to stroke it
Its little body twitched
I used to sit and wonder
'Could I be a witch?'

Then one day in the kitchen
The fly looked in my eye
I felt his body crumble
As I cooked him in my pie

The next day at the table
As we ate the pie
The little fly came back to me
And solemnly asked me, 'Why?

Why did you have to cook me?
What's the point in it?
Please put me on my window
And leave me to look and sit'

I put the fly on the window
And left it there all day
Then as I came back to the window
The fly had come to say:

'My body is broken and stiff
My wings are broken and old
Please leave me on my window
Until I turn blue and cold'

The little fly on the window
Has been there since I came
Its empty little body
Lies there all the same.

Katie Harbon (15)
The Knights Templar School, Baldock

World Unknown

Each breath I take is a new life congesting my lungs,
I am isolated by illuminous plants of all shapes and sizes
Of all colours that I'm captured and fantasised by
As they have never been discovered throughout time.

The phosphorescent petals of flowers overlook
The aqua-blue water which reflects ultra-violet beams onto my body,
Golden fireflies dance upon the enchantments of this world I am in,
My footsteps gleam beneath my feet each time I take a step
Along the treasured trees that have been standing
Overlooking the crystalloid fortress
I am lost in, for many, many years.

Whispers of this world echo in my ears enhancing me to its nature
Only made up of pure souls and spirits
Granting wishes you hold so passionately in your heart,
'I never want to leave.'
Floating mountains sail above me
As the cinnamon tanned sun glitters onto its rippled surface
Formed over historic times,
Strong vines are attached to its structure
Making it seem they have been untouched by the hands of worthy,
Strong-hearted people,
Extinct animals soar over my shoulders
Painted in patterns of life and love of their sturdy bodies
Which tell stories from past life.
I look down only to find frosted ocean waves
Colliding onto the chipped rocks, the sound releases me
The nature delights me,
However this is the world I wish for, wait for, wonder for,
A place where there is only enchantment and love,
A place where there are no worries stored,

Nevertheless you always have to wake up . . .

Athen Wilton-Wright (13)
The Knights Templar School, Baldock

In My Garden

There are trees that sway left and right,
Leaves that swirl in the night,
The green grass grows in the sunlight,
In my magical garden.

The sun shines on all that grows,
Even the grass that my dad mows,
It's his pride and joy,
In my magical garden.

In the spring daffodils shoot out of the ground,
Even ones we have never found,
Like money that lays undiscovered,
In my magical garden.

Summer makes the garden like a flowering forest,
I think it's pretty but my mum's too modest,
I spend half my life,
In my magical garden.

Autumn brings a carpet of leaves,
The squirrels hide nuts like thieves,
My cats chase them up the trees,
In my magical garden.

Winter showers the garden with snow,
Bringing round our friends and foe,
All enjoying a Christmas meal,
Watching my magical garden.

Then it comes back round to spring,
And in my head a little bell rings,
It's time to start my weeding again,
In my magical garden.

Eleana Bull (13)
The Knights Templar School, Baldock

The Beast With Wings

My head is pounding,
I'm so confused!
I lie awake in the dead of night.
My eyes gleaming
Like a beacon burning bright.
I wonder about him;
The thing, the creature,
The beast with wings!
Why does he hide so many things?

I jump,
I panic and sit upright.
I saw him by the eerie moonlight,
Buried beneath the buzzing bluebottles.
He was waiting, waiting to die!
Twenty-seven and sixty-three by his side.
The thing, the creature,
The beast with wings!
Why does he hide so many things?

Now I see him clearer;
Buried beneath the covers he lies,
An empty beer bottle by his side.
'Danger' scrawled in blood red across the door!
He lies there in agony, sprawled across the floor.
Higher and higher he climbs,
To spread his beautiful black wings and fly.
Fly, fly with the owls.
Where he longs to be, where he belongs to be.
Skellig is he, the beast with wings.

Megan Pain (12)
The Knights Templar School, Baldock

Herding In Texas

Riding through those golden fields, herding those drifting cattle.
Galloping in front to steer them around, and win the wandering battle.
But soon, a cow shall stroll off, to munch on some lush food,
But I and my Forester shall canter along, in a very positive mood,
No worries about losing the cow, for we soon take control
And then we gallop up into the woods as dark as pitch-black charcoal.
The cows all dodge and push in a fright as grey birds spook the cows,
The cows are dangerous and frightening but Forester makes sure I'm sound.
But we soon come nearer, and nearer to my wonderful secure home,
After weeks and weeks of travelling, it felt amazingly like Rome.
For sleeping for a very long time on that cold, hard, grubby floor,
It made my warm straw bed look so much better and more.
All thanks to my wonderful horse, Forester the great;
He's why we got here safe and sound and not a minute late.
He was like a father to me, who cared and took charge,
But I was also like a mother to him as I gave him my commands.
We are welcomed home warmly with cake and lots of drink,
But I go straight outside to the stables to quietly think,
And also to be with the horsy friend who I clearly loved a lot,
It was Forester my dearest, eating out of his treats pot.
We truly were the greatest team that you could ever get,
For we had herded five hundred animals at yesterday's sunset.
And since then we have learnt so many things,
Especially that Forester and I were going to be together through everything!

Emily Fisher (12)
The Knights Templar School, Baldock

Skellig

Alone,
In the darkness
I had been for so long;
I had forgotten happiness years ago,
And would have given anything to hear the sound of laughter.
My joints were throbbing,
The pain was overwhelming;
It took over my body,
Leaving me lifeless and miserable;
Isolated on the garage floor.
Surrounded by rejected cobwebs and shrines of dust,
I lay longing for company,
But was beginning to realise this was only a dream.
While forlorn, my thoughts turn to my ambition of living like I used to;
The freedom I once had,
When I could swoop among the trees;
And glide in the sunlight up high in the heavens,
My only limit the horizon.
But I had to face reality
And become grateful for the little time I had left.
Hearing the owls' undisturbed calls,
Only made me plunge deeper
Into my pit of sorrow.
I lived off things most people would only eat when dared
I would soon rot away, forgotten in the shadows.
Alone,
In the darkness;
Until one day a light.

Amy McCarthy (12)
The Knights Templar School, Baldock

Untitled

Darkness swallowed the narrow, empty path.

I walk so alone.

Buried under layers of hate,
As I walk into the unknown.

Days after days,
Alone till the end.
Never getting out,
Wishing it is all pretend.

With the whisper of the trees,
With the wind encouraging me on.
Something special is arousing,
Excitement is yet to come.

A flash of lightning,
And a clash of thunder.
Something is just beginning,
Something I am under.

The shadows come alive,
A seething snake slithers.
Chaos and havoc,
The whole ground seems to shiver.

I have made a mistake,
Something must be put right.
I have to change all this,
And bring in the light.

Kate Bennett (12)
The Knights Templar School, Baldock

Mum

She was there,
She was, I swear,
I saw her,
I heard her,
Was it a sign?
Or was it a comfort?
But why was she there?
I miss her;
I love her,
Please come back soon!
'Stay safe my angel,'
I heard you say,
'Don't be scared, I love you.'
You were wearing a beautiful laced white dress,
Please come back soon.
You spoke to me and I heard,
But after a while I forgot what happened,
I knew you were there,
And I know that you love me like I love you,
Please come back soon.
It's all 'cause I love you.
I miss your laugh, your smile and your daft remarks,
And I miss your company too,
I hope you're alright,
And I will see you very soon,
Sleep tight my shooting star.

Karen Pritchett (11)
The Knights Templar School, Baldock

The Night

The night,
The morose, sombre night,
The night is bitter, freezing
As it smacks you in the face
With a hand as cold as death.
Your face red like a flame.

The bats dance in the night,
Dashing and dancing,
Pirouetting and prancing,
In the night,
The morose, sombre night.

The children,
The upbeat, enthusiastic children,
Shouting the phrase:
'Trick or treat?'
Tonight is Halloween!
Halloween is here.

The moon stares
Blank,
As clear as a blank page,
Ready to be written on.

As comets pass,
People pray,
Halloween will return again one day.

Calum Brooker (14)
The Knights Templar School, Baldock

Me, Myself, I

Hi, this is me.
I am a person, just another ordinary person,
No different from any other . . .
As ordinary as a grain of sand among a seaside beach.
But yet I stand out like a skyscraper among a village.
I'm as loud as thunder but as soft as the breeze.
I might be confident or funny,
I might be ambitious,
But look through, as if I'm a thin glass wall and you will see,
You will see.
I may be shy or boastful or biased but . . . no one is perfect.
I have lots of different qualities, some good, some bad.
Individuals, people, us; we all have different qualities, like a bowl of fruit.
The fruits have different smells, tastes and textures.
Some people like them, others don't.
Some people like my qualities, some don't.
But yet I say about people being different, we are yet all the same.
We should be treated the same.
We are grains of sand among a seaside beach.
However we are the skyscrapers.
People, individuals, us.
That is how I describe them.
I.
Me, myself, I . . .

Harry Goddard (12)
The Knights Templar School, Baldock

Harry

There was a man called Harry
Who lived on his Larry.
He met his mate Mark
In the park
And they lived on the island of Barry.

Harry Morris (12)
The Knights Templar School, Baldock

The Garage Man

There was a man who lived in an old garage.
It was as old as the earth around it!
He sat there all day, every day
And all night, every night
With deathly grey feathers arching out of his back,
Him with his pale white mask for a face.
The dead bluebottles were his best friends.
That is the garage man . . .

One night he was moved,
Moved to nowhere,
Nowhere anybody ever went
Or even spoke of,
Of the place he went to,
To nowhere.

He only ate the Chinese takeaway,
27 and 53, add a few Paracetamol,
That was all,
All he ate.
Ale, add some cod liver oil,
Was all he drank!
As lonely as a nobody,
He is

The garage man.

Daniel Maynard (12)
The Knights Templar School, Baldock

Snap, Snap, Snap

Snap, snap, snap goes the camera
Snap, snap, snap take a picture
You can use it anywhere
The zoo, the park, a birthday and everywhere
Some are waterproof, some are not
You can take it anywhere you want.

Callum Duffy (12)
The Knights Templar School, Baldock

The Midnight Murderers

The rain was pelting down,
But that sound was clear;
Something weird was happening,
Someone bad was here!
I pulled my cover up
Right over my head,
I heard a screech and a scatter of blood
Somebody was dead!
There were murderers in the house,
I had to get out,
But I had frozen stiff
Since they had come about!
They were getting closer
My heart filled with fear,
They entered my room
Spooky footsteps walked near.
The covers were pulled back
I saw a knife, then my life was done.
The bad boys left the building
With a scatter and a run!
The creaks disappeared,
Silence fell around
There was not a whisper
There was not a sound.

Laura Overton (11)
The Knights Templar School, Baldock

The Animal Riddle

I have never walked on feet and yet I am still a deadly sniper.
I am filled with deadly chemicals that make it easy to get my supper.
I am often 6cm tall but I can rise up to make a metre.
I am aggressive like a tiger but still delicate like a feather.
And if you know what I am I must say you're very clever.

Robin Peters (12)
The Knights Templar School, Baldock

Skellig Poem

The smell of chilli wafting up into the attic,
Homely sounds of the telly; microwave pinging
Conversations between Mina and her mum.

Skellig sits quietly in the beams of the attic,
Dirty hands illuminated by the small candle
Giving off a slight warmth patiently awaiting the meal.
Mina will quickly slip up to the attic to quell the grumbling belly
Skellig imagines is roaring like a lion.

In the subtle light he sees the owl's large eyes staring at him in the
corner, keeping a gracious distance.
The house creaks and groans under the pressure
Of the lives that are dwelling within it.

Why is it that even in the silence of the attic Skellig feels deafened?
Is it the sound of loneliness, no hope or constant pain and the wait
for the end?
The end of what?
Life?
Pain?
Loneliness?
Who knows . . . only one person and that is Skellig!

Sasha Giovine (12)
The Knights Templar School, Baldock

Flowers

Flowers are for people to show them how you feel.
Flowers are for the garden standing there so still.
Flowers come out in spring.
To show you that they bring happiness and life.
Their bright colourful petals are as sharp as a knife.
But then in the winter they all die.
It will make you sigh.
Please don't fear,
They will be back next year!

Rosie Anderson (12)
The Knights Templar School, Baldock

A Poem About Skellig

Skellig sits in the crumbling shed
The dusty floor acts as his bed
Silence holds the night still
As owls search for food to kill
Hoot, hoot, hoot, Mina calls
Waiting for Michael to come to the walls.

Owls feed Skellig during the night
Until the sun comes out and gives us light
The owls fly to their nest
And Skellig lies down to rest
Through the darkness to the house
Everything as quiet as a mouse
Mina and Michael decide to bring him food
Food of the gods and ale to brighten his mood.

Whisper, the cat, is soon in the attic
Skellig is much better and looking like magic
His wings are much stronger
And his face looks younger
His temper has suddenly gone
And his wings make him glide like a swan.

Zoe Melabianaki (12)
The Knights Templar School, Baldock

My Strawberry

My red strawberry is so red and ripe,
It looks like it's been painted in scarlet red!
My strawberry is so big,
You can hold it in your hand like an apple.
My strawberry has so many seeds,
It has more seeds than the stars in the sky!
My strawberry has so many leaves,
It has more than a tree!
My strawberry's leaves are so green,
They are greener than the finest grass!

Aisling Geoghegan
The Knights Templar School, Baldock

Distance Train

I waited;
I waited so persistently,
Gradually making my way across each wooden slat.

The night was watching me,
But my eyes were filled with tears of emotions;
I couldn't see before my eyes.

Each hand washed beside my waist,
My lashes brushed against my skin,
And my feet strolled, waiting.

I was calloused with fear;
I still waited unknowingly
What was racing the wind.

In the distance far away,
A light that shines, so illuminous,
It comes and I will go.

It's coming closer I can see,
My eyes are shot as it's near,
Bang, I am down, I'm not on it, I'm under it . . .

Natalie Smith (12)
The Knights Templar School, Baldock

Limericks

There once was a curious nutter
Who tried to eat all the world's butter
He ate so much bread
It went to his head
And now his brain's all full of clutter.

I once saw an interesting horse
Who lived on spaghetti and sauce
He also liked steak
And played with a rake
He was insane of course.

Alexander Bandy (12)
The Knights Templar School, Baldock

Crime

A brick through that window,
Shoving that window,
It would never be me,

That car broken into,
That purse just got switched,
It would never be me,

That little boy stabbed,
That passport nabbed,
It would never be me,

That was him speeding,
Taking books from the reading,
It would never be me,

Watching that crime,
Them taking that wine,
It would never be me,

The phone next to me,
The crime on the streets,
I would never tell, would you?

Luke Geaves (14)
The Knights Templar School, Baldock

A Pair Of Limericks

There once was a soldier called Tom
Who died in Iraq from a bomb
He saw S Club 7
Flew up to Heaven
And then had tea with his mom.

There was a group of ladies
They all drove nice Mercedes
They had lots of dosh
And acted very posh
But none would have any babies.

George Fryer (12)
The Knights Templar School, Baldock

The Moon

Once upon a most mournful tale
There could be heard a morose wail.
Throughout the stars,
Throughout the Earth,
It was a simple cry.
An innocent question, why?
Why had she been thrown,
Banished to darkness?
Now the stars are her tears
And all she fears.
Space her exile,
Cold and empty.
She hopes, wishes, one day she might
Be allowed to bask in her sister's light.
Her glory one day redeemed,
Praised by all.
Not just lonely travellers out at midnight
Looking for some warmth in her light.
But 'til that day she'll cry tears of cosmic dust
And be thankful for those few who come to see her pure beauty.

Storm Cook (13)
The Knights Templar School, Baldock

Skellig

A mysterious man
Lies beneath the chest of drawers
On the crumbling floor covered in bluebottles,

A mysterious man,
Filled with cracks, creases and cuts,
His flat feet flopped facing under his sack-like suit,

A mysterious man,
With a face as pale as plaster and a few fine hairs on his chin

A mysterious man, called . . . Skellig.

Jody Margetson (12)
The Knights Templar School, Baldock

Snake

The snake is very slim
The snake is slimy
The snake is really slippery
But not at all tiny.

My great pet snake
I have called him Jake
I put him to bed
The next time I checked, he had fled
I looked all night
Then I heard a little bite
I brought him home
And he slept in his little dome.

The snake can travel
He can climb, but you can't see
His jelly spine
Can't make or break
Can't shake or wake
They rhyme with lake
And they are obviously snakes.

Alfie Laughton
The Knights Templar School, Baldock

Summer!

Summer is near, sort of
A few raindrops from the sky
The sun is shy today
The six week holiday is coming our way
May has been and gone
The sun has shone
And now it's a brighter day
It was brighter yesterday than today
A few more puffs appear in the sky
Then comes the rain
All over again.

Danni Malyon (11)
The Knights Templar School, Baldock

My Friends

My friends are always there for me,
They help me through my troubles,
No matter what they may be

Whether I am sad or glad,
They will be there,
We always have lots of secrets to share!

You help me through my problems,
Through things good and bad!
You help me keep smiling,
Even when I am sad.

In happiness and laughter,
In sadness and tears,
Thanks to all my friends,
I will overcome my fears.

And wherever the years take us,
No place is too far.
We will think of each other,
Wherever we are!

Sam Tomlinson (11)
The Knights Templar School, Baldock

Jack

Terrified,
He sat up, lifted his dirt-ridden feet across the trench,
The fear, sheer fear of the evil, chaos.
Bang, bang, bang.
Bullets.
He shivered; his eyes wept,
He saw the corpse's face. Jack.
It was Jack. Jack was dead.
His heart sank, but the bullets started again.
He had to get out.
He had to . . .

Rosie Lord (13)
The Knights Templar School, Baldock

Ssss What Am I?

I'm sometimes a fake
I slither around
And I love fresh steak
Although no one can see
Because I'm a ninja
Guess what I am?
I'm camouflaged
But when I'm seen
They think I am mean . . .
I'm like a ghillie sniper
In the grass
When you see me
You'll want to pass
But I'm not really that mean . . .
Have you guessed yet
What I am?
Look at your bag ma'am
That was my sister
How about your shoes, mister?

Matty Welander
The Knights Templar School, Baldock

Snake

The snake was as still as
A highly trained sniper,
As tough as a tank.
The snake's eyes were as
Blank as the moon.
The fangs of the snake are
As delicate as a princess.
The poison is as potent
As a backstabbing assassin.
The snake winds like a chasm.

Nicholas Bell (11)
The Knights Templar School, Baldock

Haikus

Gloom

The door creaks open
A gloomy mist pouring out
Really bitter cold.

The circus

The ringmaster shouts
The lion threatens to bite
Clowns throw custard pies.

Happiness

Everyone is here
Laughing and joking is fun
But happiness is best.

Africa

The tall giraffes stand
A herd of zebras stampede
The sunset is great.

Katie Winzer (12)
The Knights Templar School, Baldock

Skellig

Skellig is old, hurt, has very long wings!
He lives in a garage, but then one day
A boy and girl came along and lifted him away.

A secret garden is where he went, a place where nobody would go.
The owls fed him all day long until he was strong enough to go.

He had been living on 27 and 53 for most of his life.
Mina and Michael were his saviours.
Off he flew;
Nobody else knew.

Rosie Barker (11)
The Knights Templar School, Baldock

The Truth About A Snake

Snakes are the killers so they say . . .
Taking photographs, making TV programmes,
Hunting, entertainment, zoos, skin using,
If snakes are made out to be the killers, maybe that's why?

The snake is strong, the snake is proud,
It slithers silently through the grass,
Lurking in the sinister dark night,
The snake is a long thread of colours in the light.

But if a human disturbs its kind,
Then what can one expect?
Those great creatures just want peace,
Not to be pestered by us, on their land.

So when you ever see a film
Where the humans are getting attacked, think:
Yes it's horrible and not nice for them,
But is there more to it than just snake's actions?
What about ours?

Anna Docking (12)
The Knights Templar School, Baldock

Skellig

There is a man in a garage,
But who could it be?
An old crooked man,
But I wonder, can it be true?

It's in the darkness
With all the creepy creatures!
But, who could it be?
Brad Pitt?
Noo . . . It can't be!
Justin Bieber?
Of course not!
But I wonder . . . who is it?

Denver Tuck (11)
The Knights Templar School, Baldock

War Poem

In the past
War has arrived,
Pounced on countries
That are unprepared.

Nobody thought that such
Friendships could be made.
These foreigners stand together,
Standing strong and unafraid.

People shelter in the trenches
Like a brave frightened rabbit.
Rats like furry walking whales!
This trench of frosty hell.

War brought Hell to Earth then.
In some places, war still surfaces,
Conflict is everywhere your eyes look!
No one deserves the fire of war.

Sophie Hazzard (14)
The Knights Templar School, Baldock

The Spider

Spider in the bath,
Spider on your scarf
Spider on your bed
Spider on your head

It swings
It swoops
It scuttles
It scares

It creeps
It crawls
It climbs
It crouches.

Amelia Ellis
The Knights Templar School, Baldock

Untitled

Bullets shot, grenades thrown,
Mines set, the whistle blows,
Courageous soldiers sent over the top
Trying to foil the enemy plot.

The General's miles behind the line,
Sipping from his glass of wine,
As he leans back in his comfy chair,
The smell of death drifts through the air.

The lions wade through soft, thick sludge,
The artillery's left a pool of blood.
A life, a good friend, lost to war,
As the crows above shriek, yell and caw.

The mice send lions to their deaths,
The wind is formed from dying breaths.
The mice march their men to the end,
Who cares? They've got lots more to spend!

Aidan Tilbury & Max Johnson (14)
The Knights Templar School, Baldock

Sun

I shine down on you;
I am a light so bright I blind you!
But enjoy me while you can, I am at my best for only one quarter of the year.

From far away you enjoy me,
If you were up close I don't think you'd feel the same way!
In the morning I rise from under the dark duvet covers,
At night I pull them back over my head.

Without me there would be no you!
Nothing would be the same,
You look in the sky, how wonderful I look,
Do you know how crucial I am?

Helen Inman (12)
The Knights Templar School, Baldock

Things The Snake Does In A Day

The snake is as slow as a snail,
Its eyes glow in the evening sky
It is so quick that it can sneak up
And bite you on the back and the neck.
It is so deadly and poisonous.

It eats one mouse a day,
It slithers into the stream,
If you cover yourself with mud it will go and ignore you,
Sometimes it splats poison in your eye,
You will suddenly die.

It hates ice-cold things,
The heat gives it a holiday,
It likes music but only rock,
It lives in the dangerous jungle.

Jason Doherty
The Knights Templar School, Baldock

Skellig Poem

Skellig is a poor old man
He scavenges for food whenever he can
Day after day he sits in the garage
Hoping Michael will bring him 27 and 53
While he is waiting for Michael to come he eats the flies and deathly spiders when they crawl across his pale face
He just sits there waiting to die
He does not care about his life anymore, he has just given up on himself
His wings will never be able to grow bigger and stronger ever again they have been crunched up for years
Maybe when Michael comes again maybe Skellig won't be there
He will never be able to live his full life with arthritis and many more illnesses.

Jemma Fairey (12)
The Knights Templar School, Baldock

Skellig

Half beast, half angel with pale skin.
He is filthy, dirty with cobwebs hanging from his feathered wings.
His manners are poor,
He rejects all help;
He has arthritis.

The garage is where he lives; smelly and cluttered with junk.
Mina and Michael are friends who find Skellig behind cabinets in the garage.
Shocked at the sight of the beast.
Skellig always loves eating 27 and 53
From the Chinese menu.

The story is a mystery and very adventurous.

Jason Coyne (11)
The Knights Templar School, Baldock

Dancing Well And Off She Shops

Dancing Well
There was a young man from France
Who was busy learning to dance
He stumbled and fell
Down a very deep well
And days later woke up in a trance.

Off She Shops
There was a new girl called Pop
Who really enjoyed to shop
So she travelled away
For a week and a day
And came back with millions of tops.

Montana Strachan (12)
The Knights Templar School, Baldock

The Big Day

It's the final, it's the big day,
What's going to happen, what will happen?
England vs Spain, will it be 1-0?
Or will it be two on the big day?
It's upon us, the big day,
Spain singing, 'Go Spain.'
England fans singing, 'Go England.'
The referee goes to blow his clean whistle.
It's the big day,
Spain attack Torres with the ball at his feet,
Oh he shoots, James tips it onto the bar,
Oh it's a magnificent save.

Jake Smith (11)
The Knights Templar School, Baldock

Hot, Hot, Hot Summer

The sun bursts through the clouds.
The sparkling water winks away the day
The smell of sunscreen, like freshly made cupcakes.

The pounds spent on cheating tans,
The ringing at the tills for sunglasses being sold.
The siren of the ice cream van, and children screaming for lollies.

Lying on a sunbed, burning in the sun.
Friends having water fights, and splashing in the pool.
Having a great time, *wooaah*, this is summer!

Imogen Hornby (12)
The Knights Templar School, Baldock

Ghost Rider

The cold air wraps its grey arms around Hertfordshire.
In a graveyard, not too far from here,
The legendary ghost rider haunts.

It is now Halloween and he is preparing.
Crash, whistle, whoosh, he is ready.

He rides into the night.
Children's scared voices whistle in the wind.
He hears the screams.
A small meaningful smile!

Rajvir Singh Jagpal (14)
The Knights Templar School, Baldock

The Snake

The snake is a deadly weapon, waiting for its prey,
It slithers silently, sensing movement with its jaw.
And when it senses any, it will wait for its lunch.

The snake is smooth, but also rough,
It senses heat and picks up traces of wee until it gets to its lunch.
When it finds it, it will dislocate its jaw and eat a mouse in one.

The snake is camouflaged to hide from its prey.
Then after a week, it will look for another mouse.
And after eating that, it will wait for a week.

Stuart Dougal (11)
The Knights Templar School, Baldock

Sue's Odd Shoes

There was a young ballet dancer called Sue.
She had different colour ballet shoes.
She had a little think,
Then painted them pink,
Then they were normal ballet shoes.

Emma Nicholson (12)
The Knights Templar School, Baldock

I Had To . . .

I had to write a poem,
My teacher said.
I didn't really know what was in my head,

So here I am writing what's in my mind,
I wish I'd got this homework some other time,

And now here I am, right where I'm sat.
Hey! I made a poem,
How did I do that?

Serena Harmsworth (12)
The Knights Templar School, Baldock

Halloween

The strong autumn wind blew pure evil,
The day grew darker,
More and more scary children emerged,
Terrifying the people.

The fiery, orange glow in the window,
The pale, scary ghost,
The ding dong on the doorbell.

The strong autumn wind was blowing . . .

Carris Lee (13)
The Knights Templar School, Baldock

Diabolical Tongue Twister

Some sort of snake slithered
Slowly down the slimy slope and
Slipped sadly into the sloppy slate
Which slipped and sploshed as the
Slimy snake slithered slowly out
The slate, it slipped down the slippery
Slimy, soggy slope.

Sophie Hornblower (12)
The Knights Templar School, Baldock

Untitled

Meat always gets hung up there, the butcher's shop.
A lowly pig lies in the farm, eating slimy slop.
The man in the farm takes the pig, lanky and skinny.
Next thing the pig can see is a massive cleaver, rocketing down.

This pig was like my friend, taken from his home.
He went to school, other boys were bullying him.
Not long after, he couldn't take it any more, a car sped past
And that is how my friend died.

Joe Nelson (11)
The Knights Templar School, Baldock

Hands

Hands are for touching and writing and feeling
Hands are for picking things up
And typing on the computer
Because if you didn't have hands
You wouldn't be able to:
Eat, drink, dig, write, open doors, close doors, draw
Play instruments and the worst thing of all is
That you wouldn't be able to dress yourself.

Daisy Flynn (12)
The Knights Templar School, Baldock

Skellig

Skellig is as dark as coal.
Mina is sarcastic,
Michael is secretive.
Angels fly high.
Owls hoot in the midnight sky.
Skellig is cracked,
Mina is intelligent,
Michael is shy.

Holly Hayes (12)
The Knights Templar School, Baldock

Who Is God?

Who is God?
Is he a man or is he a myth?
Do you believe or do you care?
To me God is above.
Looking out for me and guiding my life.
To others God has different names.
Whatever you may think,
God is true to me.

Jack Smith (12)
The Knights Templar School, Baldock

The Thing

The thing I use every day
Is the best in the world and
No one wanted it, and this is why:
You can use it as a weapon, but that's boring
I use it for making music
You can even use it for playing golf
I love it, it's like a spy surrounded and gets back up
I love to drink out of it!

Michael Fairburn (13)
The Knights Templar School, Baldock

My Cat, Bumper!

My cat, my cat, how sweet is a cat?
Sitting and sleeping, how cute is that?
Playing with mice and a big ball of string,
Finishing the day with some tea,
Going outside looking for a mouse.
Her fur so black and white like snow,
She shines like the stars with whiskers
Dragging to the ground,
That is my cat.

Tamsin English (13)
Uplands Community College, Wadhurst

The Fair

The fair is getting built
And the ride is shining.
The lights are going up
And they're brightening.
Everyone's getting excited for the party
As the funny twister
Is going round and the
Lights are flashing.
So is the gravity cage.
It's white and it goes
Crazy if you let go of your gravity.
It's the funnest fair that
There's ever been.

Jade Berry (13)
Uplands Community College, Wadhurst

My Little Black Friend

As I wait for my wicked revenge,
So quiet it makes no noise at all,
Claws as sharp as razor blades
And fur as black as coal,
I live a long and happy life.

My eyes are as black as the night.
My whiskers are as long as hair.
I live way up there, among the ground down there.

What am I?

Sofie Fairweather (12)
Uplands Community College, Wadhurst

The Heart Of Battle

In the trenches with dirt and filth, men surrounding
On the face of battle, guns blazing, tanks
Rolling onto the incoming enemy.
Troops assembling at the trenches of battle,
People dying all around, people screaming in the heart of battle,
Gunfire fills up the air with sounds.
Aircraft raging above,
It all ends with a shot.

Elliott Wallis (12)
Uplands Community College, Wadhurst

Summer Is Coming

As summer enters, the flowers are blooming
The sun is in the sky
The people going to the beach
Smiling and wearing sunglasses
People sunbathing
I go cycling in the summer.

Ian Lim (12)
Uplands Community College, Wadhurst

Young Writers Information

We hope you have enjoyed reading this book - and that you will continue to enjoy it in the coming years.

If you like reading and writing poetry drop us a line, or give us a call, and we'll send you a free information pack.

Alternatively if you would like to order further copies of this book or any of our other titles, then please give us a call or log onto our website at www.youngwriters.co.uk.

Young Writers Information
Remus House
Coltsfoot Drive
Peterborough
PE2 9JX
(01733) 890066